The Reluctant Mentor

The Reluctant Mentor

The Reluctant Mentor

How Baby Boomers and Millenials Can Mentor Each Other in the Modern Workplace

By Lew Sauder and Jeff Porter

The Reluctant Mentor

Copyright © 2013 by Lew Sauder and Jeff Porter

Edited by Stephanie S. Diamond

Library of Congress Catalog Number: 2013917431

The Reluctant Mentor: How Baby Boomers and Millenials Can Mentor Each Other in the Modern Workplace

by Lew Sauder and Jeff Porter

ISBN 978-0-9830266-5-5

Additional copies of this book can be ordered from Create Space, www.CreateSpace.com, or from your favorite online bookstore.

Dedication:

Lew: Dedicated to Emily, Sam, Holly, and Heather

Jeff: Dedicated to Lainie, Dane, Holly, Jessica, Amanda, and Lori.

Acknowledgements:

Lew's acknowledgements:

I can attribute much of my success in life to the mentors that I have had. First, to my high school history teacher Darrel A. Sutter: Darrell's teaching approach to go beyond the 2x4 teaching approach (two covers of a book and four walls of the classroom) taught me that there is more to the world than the cornfields and bean fields I grew up around. Tolerance, open-mindedness, and critical thinking were interwoven in every lesson he taught.

Thank you to Michael M. Curran, my first career manager. His logical business insights and level-headed manner taught me an approach that I have tried to model throughout my career.

Perhaps the most influential mentor in my career has been R. Gibbs Vandercook. Gibbs' knowledge, advice, and story-telling abilities have combined over the years to teach me valuable lessons in business and in life.

My wife, Heather Sauder, is a teacher by trade and by nature. Her patience and persistence are a model that I strive for, though still a work-in-process.

And finally, thank you to my newest mentors, my kids, Emily, Sam, and Holly Sauder. From their perspectives, not to mention their intimacy and comfort with technology, I learn something new from them every day.

The Reluctant Mentor

Jeff's acknowledgements:

Although I have never sought a mentor, nor have I been formally asked to be a mentor to others, I have gained a great deal of insight, knowledge, and motivation from both sides of many mentoring relationships over a long and diverse career.

Some of my earliest professional mentors that I still draw experiences from are Ted Fregon, Kevin Bohan, and Graeme Burton, to whom I owe much of my formative engineering experience.

In business development and negotiation, I owe gratitude to Stephen Found, in project management and work ethic, Mike Munday. Probably the most formal mentoring relationship I have ever had was with Bob Gawne, to whom I pay regular respect through sharing of his quotes and patient advice. Steve Chetcuti deserves thanks and patience for imparting his experience with startups and entrepreneurism in general.

In recent years, Cheri Caddy and Guy Timberlake for their guidance through the complexities of business within the U.S. Federal Government.

My wife, Lori Porter, has taught me in more ways that I can recall and is always my reality check. Lainie, Dane, and Holly Porter, as well as Jessica Ray and Amanda Bliss are more than family, they are always an inspiration.

The Reluctant Mentor

Lew and Jeff:

We are both grateful for the detailed editing efforts from Stephanie S. Diamond for editing our original draft. Her grammatical knowledge, attention to detail and creative suggestions combined to help us create a much better final product. You can contact Stephanie for her services at: (https://www.facebook.com/StephanieSmithDiamond)

Thank you to Robert G. DelCampo, Ph. D for his valuable input to this subject and for providing a foreword to our book.

A special thanks to Jennifer Wells for the cover design. Her creativity and professionalism reveal the passion with which she performs her craft. You can contact Jennifer for her artistic services at http://jennifernicholewells.com/.

Table of Contents

Foreword

For the first time in history, four generations actively engage in the workforce. The reason is irrelevant. Some posit that economic conditions play a role. Others believe that the improved quality of medical care plays a role, yet others point to the Silent Generation and Baby Boomers finally achieving their lifelong dream jobs as reasons for this unique combination of workers. Regardless of the reason, the bottom line remains that we have drastically different value systems and work styles at play.

The Reluctant Mentor, by Lew Sauder and Jeff Porter provides a unique glimpse into the dynamics of two very distinct, yet complementary value sets in the modern work environment. Expertly crafted to draw in the reader, yet providing valuable insight and experience in working with multiple generations, Lew and Jeff "hit the nail on the head" and identify how generational clash is an emerging issue for today's managers.

Within the next 5-10 years, Generation Y, or as I prefer to call them, Millennials, will become an ever-present fixture in the workforce. Millennials (those with a formative experience that includes the advent of the internet, 9/11 and the cell phone as fixtures of their worldview) will become a dominant force. Many point to statistics noting that 46% of Millennials have some form of "body modification" (a visible tattoo or non-standard piercing) and scoff—"I can't have *those people* working for me, what would my customers think?" First, those are the customers of the future. Secondly, would you rather have someone with body art or someone completely unqualified? Or worse yet, close your business for good?

As a university educator and administrator, I interact with these Millennials on a day-to-day basis. The struggles that I have with "helicopter parents" and the perception of entitlement are the issues of tomorrow's workforce. However, Millennials present not only significant challenges, but great opportunity. Many believe that this group will have to change when they enter the workforce, but statistically this viewpoint is unrealistic. With a shrinking number of Generation Xers, corporations and small business alike will have to look to the millennial generation for talent, skill and innovation.

Turnover research demonstrates that those who leave the workforce are normally very high performers - leaving for better opportunities or low performers - being "managed out" of organizations. Theoretically, a firm without a strategic focus on retention of employees will have a mediocre workforce; unless of course they create unique links or somehow embed their employees in their organization through means other than the actual day-to-day work. This will ring especially true for Millennials as they value work-life balance much more than previous generations.

The Reluctant Mentor

Some view this value of work-life balance as laziness or unrealistic expectations, but perhaps this is due to careful attention to the struggles of prior generations. Maybe they have seen their parents, grandparents, aunts, uncles or others chewed up and spit out by corporate life. Perhaps they have seen a lifelong employee of a large organization have their long coveted pension squandered by the unethical choice of an arrogant CEO. Perhaps the Millennials are more intelligent than we think. They may have figured out that balance doesn't mean less work, it means less burnout!

This is but one of the lessons that might be learned via multi-generational mentoring—both in practice and in Lew and Jeff's new book. As sage older workers, we believe that mentoring relationships go only one way. That we as the older, supposedly wiser, experienced individuals in the relationship will impart some great knowledge on the younger, fresh worker with idealistic views. In reality, backed up by volumes of academic research, the true value is sometimes gained in reverse.

Robert G. DelCampo, Ph.D.
Associate Dean
Rutledge Professor of Management
Bill Daniels Business Ethics Fellow
Anderson School of Management
University of New Mexico
Editor-in-Chief, Administrative Sciences

Preface

This book is a collaborative project that brings together our experiences as management professionals through a fictional organization, Stewart Bicycle Manufacturing. In the story that follows, our characters are based on observations while working with multiple generations in the workplace and how the workplace dynamic has changed dramatically from the late 1970s through today.

The dynamics of multiple generations in the workplace are not new; each generation has experienced the entry of the intern, the apprentice, and the graduate into the work environment and we have all seen some succeed while others fail, just like in all aspects of life. At work, however, this natural order has typically been predicated by a hierarchy, or a food chain, that places older, experienced people above the younger newcomers.

In a practical sense this situation persists, but the natural order has been increasingly challenged and disrupted in ways that no previous generation has had to deal with.

Through the use of modern communication, information transparency, and availability, young entrants in the workplace are typically much more enlightened and knowledgeable about some aspects of work than their supervisors and their older peers.

Although it's a generalization, Millennials, or Generation Y (those born between the early 1980s and the early 2000s) have been raised in a somewhat nurturing and encouraging environment. It's the age of the "Trophy Kids," a term coined by author Ron Alsop, where children often only had to participate to receive a trophy; outcomes and achievement are sometimes secondary[1].

Computers, smartphones, and the ubiquitous Internet allow us to gather information, communicate, and collaborate in ways that are becoming infinitely easier. Change is constant and to generalize again, the Millennials embrace change and leverage the technology to launch themselves ahead of their older counterparts.

We have observed the friction this sometimes causes but we have also experienced the benefits of working collaboratively across generational boundaries for mutual benefit. Call it mentoring, or mutual respect for anyone you have the opportunity to work with, but every interaction is an opportunity to both impart and gain knowledge, regardless of the apparent gaps in experience.

Our experiences on both sides of the mentoring relationship are exhibited in this story. We hope you enjoy, relate to, and learn from the characters regardless of where you sit in the generational continuum.

Lew Sauder and Jeff Porter

[1]Ron Aslop, The Trophy Kids Grow Up: How the Millenial Generation Is Shaking Up the Workplace (San Francisco: Jossey-Bass, 2008).

Chapter 1 – Stewart Bicycle Manufacturing

R oger looked at his watch as he heard the knock on the door. It was 9:31. He looked up to see Phil.

"Hi Roger. Ready for the meeting?"

"You're a bit early."

"I thought you said we were going to meet at nine thirty?"

"Ann had a conflict and we had to push it back by thirty minutes. We're meeting at ten o'clock now. I sent you an e-mail."

"Oh yeah, I don't check my e-mail all that often," Phil said. "Why didn't you just text me?"

Roger crinkled his face. "I just figured you would check your e-mails."

Phil started to reply and decided to stop. "I'll just see you in a half hour."

After Phil walked away, Roger Stewart shook his head through a half-exasperated sigh. In the twenty-five years since he started Stewart Bicycle Manufacturing Company in his garage, he had always prided himself on how well he related to his employees. Back then it was just a few part-time employees that helped him with assemblies.

Roger had always been an avid cycling enthusiast. He was also into hunting, fishing, and just being in the outdoors. His mountain bike passion led him to start his business at the age of thirty. Prior to that he was employed by a large financial corporation in a management role.

His hobby for as long as he could remember was bikes. He tinkered with and fixed not only his own bikes but also those of his friends. This hobby transitioned to a business at a time when Roger was feeling out of place in the corporate world.

The company launched when he came up with a design for a mountain-bike frame that was significantly lighter and more durable than others on the market. He developed a process to make it relatively easy to produce. It was considered "state of the art" for its day and Roger made a big impact in the industry. His company grew quickly in its first five years.

When he started getting more orders than he could fill out of his small shop, he borrowed some money, rented some warehouse space and hired some full-time workers to help with assemblies and take orders. He eventually hired a sales staff to begin selling his bikes out of local bike shops.

His business grew each year. Stewart Bicycle Manufacturing Company outgrew the warehouse space within a few years. For the company's tenth anniversary, he built a new facility to include the corporate offices, the warehouse, the manufacturing plant, a showroom, and a retail outlet. Roger had forty-five employees. He was now president of a formidable company.

A few years later Mark Smith, his head of sales, suggested he get a website and sell bikes online. This was a huge jump for Roger. He had used the Internet a little and seen its popularity grow. He had also seen the infamous burst of the dot-com bubble over the previous year. Roger was a smart businessman but this melding of technology and business was new to him so he wasn't sure where to start, and he was nervous about getting into something he knew little about. Mark connected Roger with a small firm that specialized in web development; they met with Roger and within a few months they were up and running on the web.

Roger was proud of their website; he felt like he was riding the tech wave. The site proved to be very lucrative in a surprisingly short period. People were somehow finding their site--although Roger had no idea how. Sales orders began rolling in from all over the country. At one point, eighty percent of their sales were from online orders and as a result Roger had to expand the new facilities to allow for another assembly line.

Now as Roger prepared to complete his twenty-fifth year in business, he was seeing sales begin to lag. He still sold bicycles out of his small storefront attached to the manufacturing plant, but they had come to rely primarily on their online business. Online sales had been flat for the past year and he was beginning to see the numbers fall faster in recent weeks.

He called a meeting with some of his staff for a brainstorming session to see if they could come up with some ideas for increasing sales. He felt he had the right mix of talent for the meeting. Mark Smith was Roger's right-hand man. He had been with the company for thirteen years and was instrumental in helping Roger make the move to the Internet. Mark started as head of sales. Within a few years, Roger asked him to head up the marketing group. At fifteen years younger than Roger, he seemed to have a good handle on technology, which Roger lacked.

Roger's office manager, Ann Hewitt, was also a trusted member of his inner circle. She always seemed able to take a problem and explain it in words that made it simple for everyone to understand. She also never held anything back. If she disagreed with Roger, she would always let him know in terms that were just diplomatic enough that he didn't feel like she was undermining him. Maybe it was because she was only four years younger than Roger, but he seemed to relate to her better than anyone at the company.

Phil was another story altogether. Only two years out of college, he had proven himself as a valuable employee. Phil was an avid biker and fell in love with Stewart's bikes in his second year of college. A business major, he wanted to get into sales. He interned at the company as a sales associate the summer between his junior and senior years and impressed everyone, especially Roger.

Phil Sullivan was a natural at sales and his passion for cycling was palpable. There was a noticeable increase in store traffic soon after Phil started. He really had "the gift of gab" and was great with customers. He was equally popular with the girls. Although he always seemed to have a steady girlfriend, there also seemed to be no end to the female visitors to the store to "look at bikes." Everyone could see they were more interested in Phil!

In mid-October, after Phil went back to school, Roger drove two hours up the interstate to meet Phil on campus and offer him a full-time job as a sales rep upon graduation, along with a sizable signing bonus. Phil couldn't say "yes" fast enough. This was Phil's dream job and he considered quitting school on the spot to start right away. Fortunately, Roger set the condition that he had to finish his degree, fighting the temptation to drive Phil back to the office that day.

Phil started his new job the Monday after graduation. Traffic was up on the website and sales continued to increase steadily over his first year.

Because of the recent drop in sales, Roger wanted to get some fresh ideas from the team. Phil had been talking lately about social media and some new marketing ideas that he had. Roger didn't know anything about it. He knew that Phil knew a lot more about that stuff, but he was reluctant to invest a lot of money in something he didn't know anything about. Phil was a smart kid, but Roger needed to figure out a way to convince him that there was more to the bicycle industry than the Internet and technology.

Roger's Journal:

I'm anxious to meet with Ann, Mark, and Phil to discuss the slump in sales and try to figure out how to turn it around. We rely so heavily on Internet sales, but how can we increase this market when we don't really know who the customers are. I have no idea how they find us.

While Ann and Mark know the business well, I think Phil can provide some fresh ideas. He's young, which is both good and bad. He relates better to the generation that is a large part of our market. But it seems all of his ideas are technology based. I wish he'd focus more on increasing sales than just throwing technology at everything.

Chapter 2 - Frustrated Phil

Phil walked away from Roger's office shaking his head. E-mail? He wondered. Who the hell uses e-mail anymore? No wonder our sales are going down. We're living in the dark ages.

Despite his frustrations, he loved working for Roger. Roger was a great guy and Phil knew he was smart. He had almost single-handedly built this company from nothing. He knew how to get performance from a team. Roger knew the bike business too. Phil just needed to figure out a way to get him to move into the twenty-first century. Their e-commerce system is a dinosaur, he thought, and we don't have any presence on any social-networking platforms. No wonder our sales are falling, nobody knows we exist with this old style website.

It wasn't just the way Roger communicated, although that was bad enough. Roger still used a flip phone and as the president of the company he didn't even have a LinkedIn profile. But Phil's biggest frustration was Roger's reluctance to embrace technology in general.

The Reluctant Mentor

The company had a website which helped them sell a lot more bikes. But it was a primitive e-commerce site that was really nothing more than an order collection system that sends an e-mail with the client's order details. Typically staff members had to follow up with a call or several e-mails to finalize the sale and payment details.

Phil had suggested upgrading the website and using social media to enhance their online marketing efforts, but Roger didn't understand anything Phil was talking about. Instead he wanted to continue his traditional marketing efforts, which consisted primarily of advertising in cycling magazines. Phil tried to explain search engine optimization to Roger's team, but they just thought it was an effort to game the system. "Why should we bow to Google to get them to put our website at the top of the list?" Roger had asked.

"Because that's where a majority of people go to find bicycles," Phil had countered in a slightly angry and frustrated tone. It fell on deaf ears.

That night at dinner with his girlfriend, Lori, Phil began to unload his frustration with his job at Stewart Bicycle Manufacturing. "They make a great product, but they need to get with the times. If they don't, they're going to get passed up by their competition."

"They just don't seem to understand how to market in today's world," said Lori in an understanding tone. "You need to figure out a way to communicate to Roger to get him to understand how important this is to the company's future."

"You're right. It just seems so obvious. I don't understand why I need to."

Phil's Evernote:

I'm starting to get really frustrated at work. Roger and the others seem to be ignoring me and my ideas for bringing them into the twenty-first century by using social media. It seems so obvious to me! Instead Roger seems to be stuck in his traditional ways of magazine advertising and even billboards, while we have a website that was built about ten years ago. What pisses me off the most is their arrogance, like we have been doing it like this for a long time and doing okay so why should we change?

Lori raised a good point that it's up to me to get Roger to understand that this is important and can help the company, but I just don't know how to make him listen.

Chapter 3 – The Meeting

By a few minutes after ten everyone had settled in and gotten their small talk out of their systems. They could all tell that Roger was anxious to get started.

"Thanks again everyone for taking time out of your day to get together like this," Roger began. He interrupted himself as he looked back at the group. "Phil, can you put your tablet down while we're meeting please?"

Phil looked up and explained, "Oh, I'm using it to take notes for the meeting. I use an app called Evernote. It lets me take notes, file them away, and have them available to read later on my phone or my laptop."

"Okay" said Roger looking a bit annoyed. "Just try not to be too distracting. As you know, one of my biggest concerns and top priorities lately has been our drop in sales over the past year, particularly over the past quarter." He walked up to the large whiteboard on his office wall and opened a dry-erase marker. "I'd like to start brainstorming ways to increase our sales."

Phil was the first to speak up. "I think one of our key weaknesses is our website."

The Reluctant Mentor

Instead of writing the idea on the whiteboard, Roger pushed back, "What weakness do you see in our website?" he asked, somewhat defensively.

"It's very static. We show some basic pictures of our bike models, and take orders from it."

"That's really all we need it to do," Mark responded. "I think we need to do more to drive people to the website and we'll begin increasing orders."

"I agree," said Roger, writing on the whiteboard for the first time. *"Drive more customers to the website."* "That's all well and good. The tough question is how. How can we get more people to visit our website?"

Once again, Phil had an idea. "We should get more involved in social media. We should start campaigns on Twitter and Facebook at a minimum. We could pin pictures of our bikes on Pinterest and even create a YouTube channel with some videos with profiles of people who use our bikes."

"How will that drive business to our website?" Ann asked. "Will people really go to YouTube to watch videos of people riding our bikes? I also can't imagine people going to our site from Facebook while they're catching up on the activities of their family and friends."

"I agree," Mark said. "I was going to suggest we increase our advertising budget on cycling magazines. We already advertise in the top two mags. If we added another one or two to get a broader market and also increased our ad sizes, I think we could increase our penetration."

"I like that," said Roger as he wrote down as a sub-bullet under the first item. "What else will drive more traffic to the site?"

"Have you ever thought about radio spots?" Mark threw out.

Roger wrote it down. "Radio is pretty expensive, but I think it's something we should at least entertain."

Phil could feel his face getting hot. We live in the iTunes era, he thought. Nobody listens to radio anymore. He had some other ideas that he had thought about and was prepared to share with the group, but his best ideas had been summarily shot down. What was the use of sharing anymore? He sat there listening, but not participating.

Ann suggested billboard advertising. "Just because our customers ride bikes, doesn't mean they don't drive cars. They probably daydream about getting out on the bike while they sit in traffic. Billboards on the highway would be a perfect link from the daydream to our actual website."

So would a podcast, Phil thought to himself.

"That's excellent," Roger said as he wrote it down. "Let's focus on the product. Right now we offer our bikes in twelve different colors. Do you think a wider array of colors would help bump up sales?"

"How will customers know about the additional colors?" Phil threw out, breaking his vow of silence.

"Let's not worry about that right now. We're just brainstorming. We don't want to shoot any ideas down," said Roger.

Are you friggin kidding me? thought Phil, again, biting his tongue.

"I'm not big on the additional colors myself," said Ann, "but we should look into other enhancement options for the product. I don't know if that's more colors or if it's advancements in braking systems or even more comfortable seats. Mark, have you done any market surveys to see what the next big thing is that people are looking for?"

"Not lately. We did some a few years ago, but it's a little stale by now," Mark replied.

"Let's just put down 'Product enhancements' and 'Market survey,'" Roger said as he wrote them down. "Mark, we can talk later about how deep we want to delve into that."

The rest of the meeting was spent discussing traditional marketing channels between Ann, Mark, and Roger. Phil had very little to say.

Roger finally closed the meeting saying, "I'll review the options we came up with here and we'll reconvene next week sometime. Thanks to all of you for your input."

The Reluctant Mentor

As they all got up to leave, Roger asked Phil if he would stay for a minute. When Ann and Mark left, Roger closed the door and turned to Phil with a somber look on his face. "Phil, I asked you to attend this meeting because I thought you would have some better insights to increasing our sales. I was a little disappointed. You didn't say much during the whole meeting."

"Roger, I did try to contribute. I made some suggestions early on and you shot them down. Then when I asked a question, you told me not to shoot an idea down. I'm not sure what to do."

"Maybe I shouldn't have discounted your ideas like that in a brainstorming session, Phil. But you have to admit, your ideas were kind of out there. You're trying to latch on to Internet fads that I don't think are going to help us sell bikes. We need to stay grounded in reality."

Phil took a deep breath to avoid letting frustration get to him. "Roger, those ideas really aren't that far out there. And they're really not fads. They have millions of users and there are companies using them every day to sell products. I'm just trying to keep us from getting passed up by our competitors."

"I appreciate that," said Roger a little too condescendingly. "And I'm sorry if I shot your ideas down too quickly. I don't want to discourage you from participating and contributing ideas."

"Okay," said Phil, not knowing how else to respond.

"Thank you, Phil," said Roger, indicating that the conversation was over and thinking he had resolved the issue.

Phil walked out of Roger's office discouraged. He felt he had some great ideas that could really help Stewart Bicycle Manufacturing increase sales and push them to the next level. If only he could get them to think a little differently.

Roger's Journal:

I was happy with some of the ideas that came out of the team meeting today. I need to digest them for awhile before making a decision on which way to go.

I'm a little frustrated with Phil. I know he means well, but he's always trying to solve problems with technology. How do I convince him that technology is just a tool, not a magic potion that will automatically solve our problems?

Phil's Evernote:

These guys are just so far out of touch with the world. The Internet is going past them like jet fighters and they're trying to figure out the best route for their horse and buggy. We are being overtaken at the speed of sound and they can't see it.

I thought this would be a great place to work. But if they're just going to stubbornly stick to these old-school approaches, I may need to move on.

Chapter 4 – Roanoke Business Owners Network

Roger pulled into the parking lot at Amigoni's Ristorante for his weekly lunch meeting of the Roanoke Business Owners Network. Over the years, this little gathering had become the highlight of Roger's week. He had developed some good friendships and enjoyed the friendly banter with fellow business owners and bouncing various ideas off of each other.

Two of his best friends, Robb and Jon, were fellow members and he enjoyed seeing them as well. Besides, the pasta and garlic bread at Amigoni's was second to none.

The president called the meeting to order. The group swiftly marched through the formalities of meeting minutes, old business, and new business. The actual meeting didn't take too long. Once they adjourned from that, the real purpose of the group started. Besides getting a break from the traditional sandwiches at their desks, it was a chance to talk business with their fellow business owners and swap a few jokes and tall stories here and there.

The Reluctant Mentor

Once the food was served Roger turned toward Jon and asked how business was for him. Jon Franklin owned Franklin's Bakery. He had started it just a few years after Roger started manufacturing bicycles. Like Roger, he started small and gradually grew the business. At the beginning, he had a small donut shop. Within a few years, he had expanded to baking cakes and pies for special orders around the holidays. That became so popular that he invested in a larger shop and began selling them in local grocery stores in the frozen food section. When Roger added a website to his business, he and Jon had some long conversations about selling frozen desserts over the web. Jon finally decided that shipping frozen food and dealing with dry ice would be too much of a hassle. He was content expanding his network locally.

"Business is going quite well, thanks," Jon replied. "I've been in negotiations with the local warehouse club and I've got my fingers crossed that we'll be able to sell about a hundred additional items a week through them."

"How will your margins be with a warehouse club?" Robb asked. Robb Messina owned a small chain of hardware stores, the largest one being there in Roanoke. He had inherited that store from his parents. After taking it over, he modernized it and opened another store in a neighboring town. He continued a controlled expansion and had recently opened his tenth store. He was well represented throughout the central region of the state and had been able to hold his own against the big-box stores with a strategy of service and helpfulness that the bigger chain stores didn't offer.

"Margins will be lower than the rest of my distribution channels, but I'll be able to use excess capacity within the bakery, so it's a great deal."

"That's great. How are things in the bicycle business?" Robb asked, turning to Roger.

"Well, I think I've told you about our slumping sales over the past year."

Only about a thousand times, Robb and Jon collectively thought, nodding.

"I pulled together a few of my key employees the other day to try to come up with some ideas for building that back up."

"How'd it go?" asked Jon.

"Oh, I think it went fairly well. We came up with a few ideas to increase our marketing footprint and we're considering some product tweaks that could make a difference. I just have one person on my team that I'm have a little problem with."

"How so?" asked Robb.

"You've met Phil Sullivan, the guy I hired out of college two years ago?"

"Uh-huh," they both said in unison.

The Reluctant Mentor

"He's one of those kids that's always playing with technology. If he's not on a PC, he's got his phone out doing lord knows what. That in itself is issue enough. But I had him sit in on our brainstorming session. All he came up with was these crazy ideas about social media and creating videos on YouTube. I think he just wants to get the rest of our company playing on the computer instead of focusing on selling bicycles."

"I know what you mean," said Jon rolling his eyes. "I have an employee that's about the same age. I think Emily may be a couple years older. She's always got her nose buried in her smartphone texting her friends and playing games. She's been telling me to get a website and has all these crazy ideas about sending my cakes all over the world. I told her that I considered it and it just won't work, but she won't give up."

"I get the same thing," Robb added. "I have kids telling me that I should sell my products on the web. I try to tell them that's just not the type of business we're in. All those bigger stores do that, but we focus on the customer. We give advice on how to install the products they buy and make sure they buy the right item for the job. You can't do that on the Internet. Kids just don't understand the business side of it. They just want to put everything out on the Internet."

Roger looked like a light bulb went on over his head. "You know Robb, that's an excellent point. Phil's a really smart kid. And he knows a lot about bicycles. But I think I need to work with him a little and teach him more about the business side. I don't know if I took into account how green he is. Maybe if I just coached him a little and shared my years of business experience, he'll start to get it."

"I don't know," Jon said shaking his head. "These kids are so hooked on the technology, I don't know if they'll look up, or focus long enough to listen."

"You may be right," Roger said. "But I'm going to give it a try."

Roger's Journal:

I've come to the conclusion that the problem with Phil may lie less with him and more with me.

I need to teach him about the bicycle business. Once he starts getting a better understanding of the inner workings and our strategy, I think he may start coming around.

Chapter 5 – The Plant Tour

Roger gestured to a small group of workers and announced, "Here is where the actual bicycle assembly takes place." He was in his element and enjoying every minute. Roger loved giving plant tours to customers, vendors, and pretty much anyone who was interested in spending an hour hearing about how bicycles are made.

Today's tour was being presented to Gene Upshaw, a representative of a bicycle rim manufacturer from Oregon. Flanked by Mark and Phil, Roger showed Gene how each step of the assembly was performed and made sure to show him all of the quality checks they do at each station.

About mid-way through the tour, Roger looked back to notice Phil with his smartphone out, sending a text. As soon as he got Mark out of earshot from Gene, he grabbed his arm and said, "Phil has to learn to keep his nose out of that phone when we're giving guests tours."

Mark nodded, not wanting to make a big deal in front of their vendor.

The Reluctant Mentor

Later that day, Mark stopped by Roger's office. "Have you got a minute?" he asked from the doorway.

"Sure, what's up?"

"I just ran across a website I wanted to show you." He went to Roger's laptop and entered a URL. "This is the website for The Spoke Hub. It's a competing online bicycle company. Take a look at their website. They actually have a lot of things that Phil has been talking about."

About the time he said that, Phil showed up at Roger's door. "Hi, am I interrupting anything?"

"Come on in," Roger said. "I actually wanted to talk to you. Have a seat."

Phil sat in one of the chairs across from Roger's desk.

"During the plant tour, I noticed that you were texting someone. I would rather you didn't do that when we have guests present. I think it's unprofessional and just gives us a bad reputation. It's not the impression I want to give a visitor."

"Sorry about that Roger. That's actually what I came in here to talk to you about."

"Oh?" Roger smiled, thinking Phil saw the error of his ways and came in to apologize.

"Yeah do you remember when we talked to Burt Johnson? He owns that small chain of bike shops upstate."

"Yes. We never heard back from him. I thought we had lost the business."

"Well, I started talking to him again a few weeks ago. He texted me during the plant tour and said he wanted me to call him. I was texting him back to arrange a call after the tour."

"Oh," said Roger, with a significantly less smug look on his face.

"So I called him back after the tour," Phil continued. "He wants to sell our whole line at each of his stores."

"That's terrific news," Mark broke in.

Swallowing his pride, Roger said, "That is great news Phil. I'm sorry to scold you about texting now that I know what was going on. But I still would like you to step away to do something like that if we have guests around." Changing the subject quickly, he added, "Mark was just showing me this website of our competitor's. Come around here and take a look."

Mark resumed his web tour as Phil moved to the other side of the desk. "I assume you've seen this website, Phil. They have a lot of things that you suggested for our site. They have the social media links and a blog on biking. If you go into the blog, they've had a lot of people leave comments about their experiences with their bikes. Is this where you got some of your ideas Phil?"

The Reluctant Mentor

"I haven't been to this site. But these are fairly common attributes on modern websites. I have a blog on biking that gets a fair amount of traffic. I actually recognize some of the users that have comments here from my blog."

"You have a blog?" Mark blurted out in surprise.

"Can one of you tell me what a blog is?" said Roger, finally rejoining the conversation.

"A blog is short for web log," said Mark. "Why do you have a blog?" he said sharply to Phil, then without waiting for an answer he turned back to Roger and explained, "It's kind of an informal way of posting opinions or start discussions online. It allows people who read it to make comments about it."

"Can you show us your blog Phil?" asked Roger.

Phil grabbed the keyboard and entered the URL for his blog and showed it to Roger and Mark. Mark immediately began browsing through the posts. "You've got a ton of comments here. Have you ever checked the statistics on what kind of readership you get?"

"I haven't checked in a few weeks, but I was getting about a thousand hits a day."

"A thousand hits a day?" Mark repeated. "I can't believe you haven't said anything about this before?"

"Well I --"

Roger cut Phil off in mid sentence. "How many hits do we get on our website?" Roger asked.

Mark smiled. "We're lucky if we get that many in a week. We generally get between a hundred and 150 a day."

Phil's Evernote:

Today was a good day. After Roger chewed my ass about texting during a plant tour, it kind of felt good to tell him I was selling a bunch of bicycles. I also think I opened his eyes to the kind of traffic they could get if they updated their website. I could tell they were impressed with the traffic I get on my blog compared to what they get for their company site. I'm going to use that as an argument some day in the near future.

Roger's Journal:

I got pretty frustrated with Phil today. He was texting someone while we gave one of our vendors a tour. I came to learn that he was making a big deal with a customer I thought we had lost. I guess he showed me. I also learned that one of our competitors already uses most of the Internet techniques that Phil has been trying to get us to do. Maybe I'll have Mark look a little deeper into it.

Chapter 6 – Follow-up with Jon & Robb

The Roanoke Business Owners Network meeting was called to order promptly at noon. The attendees endured the business portion of the gathering. Roger was more anxious than usual to continue his conversation from last week with Jon and Robb.

As soon as the food was served he started in. "Remember last week when we were talking about the younger generation's addiction to technology?" They both nodded while chewing. "Well I had an eye-opening experience the other day."

"What happened?" Jon asked.

Roger relayed his story of the plant tour and how frustrated he got with Phil using his phone. They both rolled their eyes in exasperation. Then he told them about Phil's visit to his office. When he got to the punch line that Phil was communicating with a customer and had made the big sale, Jon shook his head, "If I were a betting man, I would have bet that he was texting one of his pals."

A knowing smile appeared on Robb's face. "Actually, these kids will surprise you every once in a while. I was in one of our stores the other day and saw one of my clerks texting on his phone. I went up to him right away and started reprimanding him about it. Then he tells me it was a customer asking a question about how to apply the fertilizer he had just bought. The clerk gave him his personal number when the customer bought it in case he had any questions."

"I don't know," said Jon. "I think it still looks bad when they're using their phone out on your retail floor like that."

"Well, I thought about that. I talked about it with our store manager here at the Roanoke site. He set up a special text message line. People take shifts monitoring it during business hours. He put the number on our website and has signs in each store announcing that customers can send a text message to ask questions about our products and services."

"How is it working out?" asked Roger.

"It's only been in place a few days, but we've already gotten about twenty texts asking questions. It's a pretty inexpensive way to increase our service and give advice to our customers."

"How much web traffic do you get on your website?" Roger asked Robb inquisitively, going off on a quick tangent.

"I haven't checked in a while, why?"

"Well it's not something that I've ever paid close attention to. But Phil has a website called a blog where he writes articles about biking. I learned yesterday that he gets more hits on his site than we get and we've been on the Internet for over ten years. He's been making suggestions for our website for a while now and I've kind of pooh-poohed them. Now I'm starting to see our competitors doing some of the same things that he's been suggesting. I'm just starting to wonder if maybe his ideas are more valid than I thought."

"I know what you mean Roger," Robb agreed. "I never would have thought anyone would send us text messages for advice. I figured if someone had a question, they'd just call us. But sometimes these kids come up with ideas we never would have thought of."

"I think the interesting message here," added Roger, "is that sometimes these kids are actually doing business when we think they're just chatting it up with their friends."

"Maybe so," said Jon. "But I still think it looks bad when they have their faces in their phones in public like that."

"I agree," added Roger. "I intend to talk with Phil. I appreciate that he was so responsive with our big new customer and helped us win business. But he needs to understand the perception issue."

Chapter 7 – A Mentoring Moment

Roger was glad to see Ann's car in the parking lot. There were very few decisions he made without bouncing them off of her. It was her combination of level-headedness and willingness to tell him the truth regardless of what he wanted to hear that made her one of his trusted advisors.

He stepped into her office and asked if she had some time to talk.

"I've had an interesting couple of days," he said as he took a seat across from Ann. He told her about Phil's texting during the plant tour, his frustration, and his subsequent realization of what Phil was actually doing. He then described his exchange with Robb and Jon at lunch.

"So what it comes down to Ann is that I think Phil is a smart guy. There's no doubt about that. He just seems a little rough around the edges business-wise. I'd like to work with him to make sure he understands some of the basic etiquette and professionalism that goes with working in the business world."

The Reluctant Mentor

Ann sat there listening to Roger without interrupting. When it appeared that he was done, she asked, "If you sat down with Phil right now, what would you say to him? What are the first things you would work with him on?"

"I'd probably start talking to him about the appropriate places to use his phone. If you get a text like that and you're with an important vendor or customer, excuse yourself and go somewhere where you can reply privately. I want to impress upon him the importance of perception. How bad it looks to a visitor when he's more focused on his phone."

"What other improvements would you like to see in Phil?" Ann asked.

"I'd like to just work on his behavior for now. Like I said, he's a smart kid. I just think he needs a little help."

"So what you're talking about is mentoring Phil?"

Roger put both hands up toward Ann. "Oh no. I'm not a mentor. We're not a big enough company to have a mentoring program. I just want to help him mature a little, that's all."

Ann shrugged. "You can call it whatever you want, "she said, "but technically, you're mentoring him. It doesn't need to be a formal program."

"I suppose you're right, I just never really thought about it that way."

The Reluctant Mentor

Ann turned to face Roger squarely, "Roger, I think you're intentions of helping Phil are good. I agree that he could use some help. But here's my opinion. I think I understand Phil. My kids are about his age. Their generation is much different from ours. They want to contribute and be part of the solution. They want to be listened to. I would suggest you go in with an open mind to also hear his ideas. Find out why he's making the suggestions he makes and let him know that you'll consider them."

Roger nodded. "That's good advice. Thanks Ann."

Roger found Phil on the sales floor. He smiled when he saw him punching his thumbs rapidly into the keyboard of his phone. "Another multi-million dollar sale?" he asked as walked up to Phil.

Phil looked up. "Oh, no, just making some notes for a blog," he responded.

Roger silently wondered what was wrong with a notepad, but dismissed the idea. "That's kind of what I'd like to talk to you about. Do you have a few minutes to talk in my office?"

In the comfort of his office Roger started in, "I want to start out by apologizing to you. In our meeting last week, you came up with some suggestions for increasing our sales and I kind of discounted them."

"Thanks," Phil said with a satisfied smile.

"I also wanted to talk to about your texting on the plant floor the other day when we were giving our vendor a tour. Now, I realize you were in the process of making a pretty big sale for us. I appreciate that and don't want to downplay it in anyway. I just want to talk about the perception it might have given in front of our guest."

"Do you think he even noticed?" asked Phil.

"I don't know. But that's not the point. If we had been giving a potential customer a tour and they noticed you texting, no matter what the purpose was, they might have gotten the impression that we're not focused on them. When we have a guest visit us, whether it's a vendor, a customer, or anyone else, we want them to think that they are our number one priority. Does that make sense?"

"Yeah, I understand that. Let me ask a question though. This customer texted me the other day because it was kind of urgent. His other bike vendor backed out of his deal and he needed the order right away. I was able to make the deal because I responded quickly. How would you suggest I should have handled it?"

Roger thought for a moment and said, "I would suggest that you tell our guest you had an urgent request come up and excuse yourself. If you went somewhere else to respond to them, no one would have seen you texting him. My issue isn't that you responded to the customer's text. It's that you did it in front of our guest. Like me, he didn't know if you were making a sale or arranging to meet your friend for a beer."

"I wouldn't have done that during a tour Roger."

Roger smiled. "I'm glad to hear that. You just have to realize that I didn't know that at the time and neither did our guest. It's easy to jump to false conclusions when we don't know."

"I understand. So... am I in trouble?" Phil asked.

"No, I'm not reprimanding you. Actually it's quite the opposite. I see a lot of potential in you Phil. You're one of the most talented people I've seen in a long time. You just have to realize that you're fairly new to the business world. I've been around the block a few times. I've made a lot of mistakes and learned from them. I just thought I could share some of my experience with you to try to help with your success."

"That's fine," said Phil.

"Let's make a deal here, Phil. I'll try not to shoot down your ideas anymore. I'll hear you out and be more of a sounding board. But whenever I can share some knowledge with you, I'll pull you aside and try to give you some business advice when I think it's necessary. I'll do it when it's just the two of us so no one else is around. We'll call them 'mentoring moments.' When I do this, I don't want you to feel like I'm shooting down your idea. I'm just trying to share my experience with you."

"Sounds like a good deal to me," Phil responded.

Roger got up and walked Phil to his office door, patting him on the back as he walked out. When he sat back down at his desk, he smiled in self-satisfaction.

Roger's Journal

I feel like I'm making headway with Phil. Although I didn't originally see it this way, Ann has pointed out that I'm mentoring him. I hope I'm able to share some of my business experience and shape him into the business person I think he's capable of being.

Phil's Evernote

Roger thinks he's mentoring me. It would have been nice if I had had some say in it. I didn't ask to be mentored. He wasn't too condescending, but I hope he doesn't start taking this mentoring thing overboard. It could really turn out to be annoying.

Chapter 8 – Roger's Realization

Mark stood in Roger's doorway. "Hi Roger. I saw your e-mail. You wanted to see me?"

"Come on in, Mark. Thanks for stopping in," Roger said, pointing toward the chairs across from his desk. "Have a seat. I had some questions for you."

Mark took a seat. "What's up?"

"Remember our competitor, The Spoke Hub? I've been looking at their website. Their blog has some good information on it. And I'm amazed by the number of people who have commented on these articles. I can't see what kind of numbers they have for hits, but if the comments are any indication, it looks like they get a lot."

Mark smiled a wry smile. "Are you starting to adopt a *Phil*-osophy on technology?"

Roger raised an eyebrow to acknowledge Marks pun and shook his head, "No, I'm just a little intrigued by some of this stuff. Hearing about the number of hits Phil gets on his young site and seeing this site by one of our competitors has got me wondering if maybe we aren't a little behind, that's all."

The Reluctant Mentor

"Well, it's a lot like our retail store. Just having traffic doesn't necessarily translate to sales, but the more traffic we can get, the better chance we have of selling. It works in a similar way with the website."

"They also have these links to Facebook and Twitter," Roger said. "My wife is on Facebook. She uses it to keep in touch with family and friends. She's always showing me pictures of my nieces and nephews. I don't understand how that can be used to sell bicycles."

Mark walked around Roger's desk so he could see his laptop screen. "If you have a Facebook account, you can click on their Facebook link and like them."

"What do you mean 'Like them'?"

"It's a way of becoming one of their followers. They're connected to you on Facebook and can send you discounts and updates on their products."

Roger shook his head. "We spend thousands of dollars on recording technology so we can record TV shows to fast-forward through the commercials. But when we go online, we invite companies to advertise to us?"

"Something like that," said Mark as he realized the irony. "I have a lunch meeting. Did you want something else?"

"No. I wanted to know what you knew about these links and how they work. I think I understand what they do, I just don't understand why people would use them. I have to go, too. I'm supposed to have lunch with Ann," Roger replied as he grabbed his coat and walked out of the office with Mark.

Ann crossed her arms and looked at Roger as the waiter took their menus and their orders to the kitchen. "Maybe I should have gotten an airplane ticket for this lunch," she commented.

Roger glanced at her, "Why is that?"

"Because you seem to be a million miles away."

Roger looked at her sheepishly. "Busted. Sorry, I've been thinking about all of this online technology stuff that Phil has been talking about. I've been looking at what The Spoke Hub is doing on their website and quite frankly, it scares me a little."

"I know what you mean. I look at how my kids use technology and sometimes I feel like the world is just passing me by."

"How are they using technology?" Roger asked.

"They're actually pretty savvy shoppers. The other day I was in a clothing store with my daughter. She saw a scarf she really liked. Instead of just buying it, she pulled out her phone, did an online search for it and found the same one at half the price. She ordered it right there in the store on her phone and we left."

Roger cringed. "That scares me. Maybe we shouldn't allow people to use their phones like that in our shop."

"I don't think that's the answer. What's to stop them from doing it out in the parking lot?"

"I suppose you're right," said Roger, shaking his head. "I expect customers to comparison shop, but I don't want them doing it right in our store."

"There shouldn't be anything wrong with it if you've got a superior quality product at competitive prices. The point of this is that this generation is our biggest market. They're in college or just graduated and working in the business world. They're the ones out there buying bicycles."

"I suppose you're right," said Roger, deep in thought.

"More importantly," Ann added, "they are much more informed and consumer savvy than we were at the same age because of the way they use technology."

Roger nodded again, he was now lost in his own thoughts.

"But Roger," Ann continued, "our response can't be to fight it. If we want to tap into this market, we need to learn more about how they shop and adapt to it."

A light bulb went off inside Roger's head. "You know Ann, you're absolutely right. I've been fighting this, thinking Phil was just coming up with crazy ideas. But the more I hear from my business owner network and from you and

Mark, the more I think we need to adapt to it. This generation is definitely different. And it's not that they're better or worse than the rest of us, just different. Maybe we need to market to them differently too."

Roger's Journal:

I'm starting to see that the world is changing around me. And if I want Stewart Bicycle Manufacturing to have continued success, I should probably change with it. I just don't know where to start.

Chapter 9 – Phil Gets His Day

Thanks for getting together on short notice folks," Roger said to the team. "I wanted to reconvene our little think tank to revisit our sales and marketing ideas from last week."

Ann and Mark were leaning in and nodding as Roger addressed them. Phil sat deep in his chair with his arms folded. He hadn't spoken a word, but his distant stance spoke volumes.

Roger continued. "When we talked last week, Phil had some ideas and I have to admit that I didn't give them proper attention. Phil, I apologized to you but I'd like to make it official in front of the rest of the team. I've become a little more enlightened since then and was wondering if you'd be interested in revisiting those ideas."

Phil unfolded his arms, sat up, and smiled. "Thanks Roger. I've been thinking about my suggestions from last week and after looking at our competitor's website, I was thinking there might be some small things we could do that wouldn't be very costly at all."

"I'm all for that," Roger responded. "What do you have in mind?"

"For starters, would you consider posting my blog on your website?"

"Sure. I've read some of your posts. They're pretty good. Mark knows the firm that makes occasional changes to the site. We can have them add it. But I have a suggestion. Just taking your blog content doesn't seem fair. How about if I buy your existing content from you? Then we'll allow you time each week as part of your job to write new posts."

Mark and Ann nodded while Phil smiled. "That's a hard deal to argue with. Thanks Roger. I was also thinking that we could create Twitter and Pinterest accounts and a Facebook page. You can do all that essentially for free. We'll need to pay our web development firm to add the links, but if we post links for each of those accounts on the website, we can start getting followers and Facebook friends."

Roger put both hands up in a surrender gesture. "Okay, okay, slow down, you're going to have to help me on that one. Why do we want that?"

"It's all about creating a community," said Phil. "We won't be hard selling them on our bikes. We'll give them information about bikes or maybe cycling events that are scheduled in various regions. When I publish a new blog post we can tweet it and put up a Facebook post pulling people into it. This all creates more traffic to the site. People will start commenting on the blog posts, retweeting our tweets and making comments on our Facebook posts."

"You said that this is free. How much time will it take from your normal work?" Ann asked.

"I will have to spend some time each day monitoring it, but other than that it's free. Another thing I think we should do is create some videos. We could do a professional-looking video for a couple hundred dollars. Maybe they interview you and show you biking. We could even do a virtual plant tour on video to show customers our quality check points."

"Okay, so all of this will involve minimal investment. Can you tell me how all of this will sell bikes?" Roger asked.

"It's probably easier to show you." Phil opened his laptop and plugged Roger's projector cord into it. When his screen image appeared on the wall, he entered the website for Dmitri's Bike Parts. "This is an online store that I've visited to shop for bike parts. See how they have links for the various social media sites?" he asked. The others nodded.

"I liked this store on Facebook a few weeks ago." Phil opened another tab in the browser and brought up the Facebook page. When he logged on, his Facebook feed appeared on the wall. As he scrolled down he explained, "Since I liked them, they send me occasional updates on specials they're running, new blog posts they've posted, and various bike racing events that they sponsor."

Roger cocked his head to one side. "So liking a company on Facebook is inviting them to send ads to you. I've always tried to avoid advertisements."

"If they totally spam you with ads you can unlike them," Phil explained. "But if they only send occasional ads and they inform me about a sale or free shipping, I'm likely to click on the link to go to their website. And like I said, sometimes they're not trying to sell me anything. This one tells me they have a new blog posted on bicycle chain maintenance."

Phil clicked on the link to show the blog post. "I may just go to the blog, read it, and leave. But it keeps Dmitri's Bike Parts top of mind. Next time I need some parts, I'm more likely to think of them and go to their website."

The others nodded in understanding. "See these share icons?" Phil continued. "If I think this is an article that would interest people in my network, I can share it on any of these social media sites." Phil clicked the share icons for Twitter and Facebook. He then switched back to the tab to display his Facebook page. "Now you can see on my Facebook page that I've shared this article for all of my Facebook friends to see."

Without waiting for a response, he opened another tab and logged on to Twitter. "You can see the same thing in my

Twitter feed. I have seven hundred and twenty-four followers. Each of them will see that I shared 'How to Maintain Your Bike Chain.' Let's say they read it and share it with their network, and some of their friends do the same thing, and so on and so on, the article can go viral. The more people who like the article, the more followers Dmitri's is likely to get. Then, when they put up a post about a special sale, it's going directly to people who are interested in their store."

Roger smiled and nodded. "I'm starting to understand this a little better."

"This all creates more traffic to the website," Phil continued. "It's about being part of the biking community. There's no one single attribute that will increase sales. It all works together. Fundamentally we are building a relationship with the customer and developing trust so that when they are ready to purchase they will think of us."

Ann jumped in. "You mentioned videos. How does that fit into the mix?"

Phil went back to the tab displaying the website for Dmitri's Bike Parts. "Remember that blog about cleaning the bike chain? Here's a video demonstration." He clicked on the video thumbnail. "Notice that it actually takes me to YouTube? If I had never heard of Dmetri's I might have gone to either Google or YouTube and searched for a video of how to clean my chain. I would have found the video through that route and then maybe I would have gone to their website from there."

Roger was tapping the keys on his own laptop and said, "I'm looking at the website for our competitor, The Spoke Hub. They're located in Madison. That's just an hour away. We should go up there and check them out."

"Do you think they would let you in?" Phil asked.

"They don't know that I'm a competitor. I just want to browse their store."

"They don't have a store," Phil explained. "At least not a brick and mortar store. They only sell online. The location in Madison is probably just a warehouse that they do their distribution through."

Roger nodded a little sheepishly. Then, changing the subject, he turned to Phil and asked, "If I give you a five-hundred-dollar budget would that be enough to get you started?"

Phil smiled. "Give me five hundred dollars and a couple of months and you won't be disappointed," he replied.

"Okay, then it's a deal," said Roger. "I'm putting you in charge of social media. Create the accounts and videos and have them posted on our site within sixty days. Mark, can you connect Phil with Web Page Solutions to have these changes made to the website?"

The marketing director responded with a nod and a terse "Will do."

Mark and Ann left the room ahead of Phil. As Phil left the room he turned to Roger and said, "See, even I can give you a mentoring moment once in a while."

Roger returned a friendly laugh in response. But after Phil was out of the room, the comment hit him. Part of him knew that Phil was right, but a bigger part of him thought it was a pretty bold statement. Who the hell are you thinking you can mentor me, he thought. Roger decided to let it go, but it left a bad taste in his mouth.

Phil had a noticeable spring in his step when he left Roger's office. He didn't get everything he had originally wanted, but he was softening Roger up enough to give some of his ideas a try. Hopefully it was just a matter of time.

Phil's Evernote:

I think Roger is coming around. I've only scratched the surface, but he's agreed to dip his toe into social media and post my blog on his website. I'm going to make sure to track the traffic so I can show him how it increases with these new ideas.

Roger's Journal:

I've decided to give Phil a chance with his ideas. This could be as much of a lesson for him as it is for me. If these ideas don't generate sales, it will show him that technology isn't always the answer. I've allocated five hundred dollars for this experiment. Even if it fails, we'll all have a little fun making some videos and Phil will learn a valuable lesson.

Chapter 10 – Phil Goes into Action

Roger was removing his bicycle from the bike rack on the back of his SUV when he noticed Phil getting out of a nearby car. "Good morning, Phil. It looks like a beautiful Saturday morning for filming."

"Hi Roger. It sure does. This is Lori."

"Hi Lori. I hear you're pretty good with the camera," Roger said, extending his hand.

Lori smiled and blushed a bit as she shook Roger's hand. "I majored in photojournalism in college. I've produced some YouTube videos for a couple of local businesses, but I don't know if I can call myself a professional yet."

"You're getting an hourly rate from us," said Phil in mock defense.

Roger laughed. "Well it's nice to meet you, Lori. What did you want to record today?"

Lori pulled out a folder and laid out some papers on the tailgate of Roger's SUV. The papers showed a storyboard for the video. "Phil wants to make the first video about you. On

Monday, we'll record an interview of you talking about your bikes. Today we want to get some action footage of you riding your bike on some of the trails here in the forest preserve," she said, pointing to the middle section of the storyboard.

They spent the next ninety minutes recording several takes of Roger riding his bike on the forest preserve trails. Lori experimented with various lighting angles where the sun shone through the trees. There was a lake about a half mile into the woods that provided an excellent backdrop to show Roger cycling.

When they finished, Lori thanked Roger for his patience. "The pleasure was all mine," Roger replied. "I felt like Steve McQueen being directed for a blockbuster action movie."

Lori laughed, making a mental note to Google who Steve McQueen is.

Lori and Phil were back at it Monday morning at seven-thirty. They had most of the lights and cameras set up in Roger's office when he arrived.

"Well, good morning again." Roger said with a smile.

Phil and Lori greeted Roger and explained how they wanted to interview him while he settled in to his workday. "I thought we could use this section of the bookshelf as a backdrop," Lori explained, pointing to the section with Roger's trophies and ribbons he had won for both business and biking accomplishments. "That really portrays your image of a successful person," she said. Roger nodded in agreement.

Lori continued, "It wasn't necessary Saturday while you were riding, but we should put some makeup on you today to avoid too much glare from the lights."

Roger displayed uneasiness about this, but agreed in silent reluctance. Although the interview went about thirty minutes beyond the planned hour, Roger enjoyed the novelty of being interviewed about his company. Lori asked some good, open-ended questions that prompted him to tell the story of how Stewart Bicycle Manufacturing began and how it evolved to a medium-sized company with small-town values. She explained that rather than turning it into an interview, she wanted it to appear that it was just him talking about the company. She would intersperse clips of him riding while he spoke.

Roger liked the concept although he wasn't sure anyone except some of his cronies from the RBON lunches would be interested in it.

When Lori felt they had enough interview footage she wrapped things up. "Phil mentioned that he wanted to do a second video that was kind of a virtual tour of the plant. Is there a day that's better than others to do some filming in the plant? We want a day where you have enough work to show the place in action, but not so busy that the place looks cluttered and disorganized."

Roger checked his production schedule. "Friday is our lightest day. There should be enough work to show a working plant."

"That sounds great. Can I come by around nine o'clock?"

"Sounds good," Roger replied.

The following Thursday, Roger called the team together for a status update. As they got down to business, he asked "Where do we stand with our online efforts Phil?"

Phil had the company website projecting on the wall from his laptop. He proudly announced that Stewart Bicycle Manufacturing now had a Twitter account, a Pinterest account, and a Facebook page. He displayed each presence on the wall and showed the team some of the things he'd posted on each account. "We only have a few people following us on each of these accounts," he explained. "But as we post more blog updates and get these links and the blog loaded to the website, that number should begin to grow."

"You're making great progress, Phil." Ann commented. "Where do we stand with the videos?"

Phil smiled. "I'm glad you asked that." He swapped the screen over to a YouTube page and began playing a video. "Lori has edited a first draft of the video featuring Roger."

As the video played Mark and Ann both smiled, taking great joy in the embarrassment Roger showed, seeing himself on the screen. "Do you have any idea how much flack I'm going to take at my networking lunches?" he asked with a smile.

When the short video ended, Phil continued. "Lori has a few finishing touches she wants to make. She'll also be here tomorrow morning to record a virtual plant tour."

"Thank you, Phil," Roger said. "Can you fill us in on your planned timeline and where you stand with your budget?"

"I don't really have a timeline. As soon as we finish all of this, we'll have the web development company post it all."

Roger frowned. "You haven't worked out a schedule for when the videos will be done and everything will be ready to put on the website? I would imagine the programmers are going to need some kind of lead time to make those changes."

Mark spoke up for the first time. "They usually want at least two weeks warning for any work. And they'll want a summary of the changes so they can estimate how long it will take to make them and have it up in production."

"I didn't realize that. I just figured we could call them when we were ready to make the changes," said Phil, rather naively.

"Alright, let's table that for now," said Roger, trying to avoid any further embarrassment for Phil. "How about your budget, where do you stand with the five-hundred-dollar budget?"

"I'm not sure about that either," Phil responded. "I don't know how many hours Lori has put into this."

"You'll also have to include the work for Web Page Solutions," added Mark. "Last time we used them I think it was around sixty dollars an hour."

Phil winced. "I had forgotten about that."

"Okay, Phil," Roger interjected. "For next week's meeting I'd like you to put together a plan that includes a timeline for when each item will be completed. Additionally, I want you to create a budget. It can be as simple as a basic spreadsheet that shows how you're spending the money and whether you're on track or not."

"Okay," Phil said, not wanting to exhibit his ignorance any further.

As the team filed out, Roger asked Phil to stick around. Roger closed the door. "I wanted to have another 'mentoring moment' Phil. If you run a project of any size-- especially one that has a budget-- you should have a plan in place that includes a timeline. When you report status, it's great to show all the things that are getting accomplished, but you should also be able to report whether you're tracking to the timeline and the budget."

"That makes sense, Roger. I'll put that together for you."

The Reluctant Mentor

"Thank you, Phil. And by the way, you're doing a great job. I like what you and Lori are doing with the videos and you got those accounts created quickly. Keep up the good work."

"Thanks, Roger," Phil managed to get out. He walked away from Roger's office a bit deflated. He had been hoping for a more positive response from the team.

Roger's journal:

I have the feeling that Phil wasn't very receptive to my advice. Phil heard me and said that he'd do what he was told. But I could tell that he didn't like what he heard. I think I'll bounce it off of Ann. Conveniently, we're scheduled to have lunch this afternoon for our bi-weekly one-on-one session.

Chapter 11 – Roger's "Ah-ha" Moment

They dined at a new upscale Italian restaurant in town. Roger didn't like the food as much as his lunches at Amigoni's and felt he was paying a lot for atmosphere and presentation, but he had given Ann the choice and he vowed to live by it. He did have to admit that their tiramisu was exquisite and he took full advantage of the dessert while Ann simply enjoyed an espresso.

"I had an experience with Phil this morning that I wanted to discuss with you," he started out.

"Since our meeting today?" Ann asked.

"Immediately afterwards. You and I had talked about me mentoring Phil. I've actually been working with him. After our meeting today you heard me ask Phil to stick around. I had what we've been calling a 'mentoring moment.' I've been giving him business advice and suggested that he develop a budget and timeline that he can report against for these efforts he's working on."

"That sounds like good advice," Ann responded. "How did he respond?"

The Reluctant Mentor

"Well that's what's kind of bothering me. He responded that he'd work on those things. I just got a bad vibe from him. It wasn't like he didn't see value in it or anything like that. What I really think is that he didn't like me telling him what to do. I'm the owner of the company. I damn well ought to be able to tell him what to do."

Ann smiled one of her wise and knowing smiles and paused just for a moment. "You're dealing with a new and unique generation of people here. I remember when my son played park district baseball. At the end of the season, every player on every team got a trophy."

"What was the trophy for? What did the winners get?" Roger asked.

"There weren't any winners," Ann replied. "Or rather, everybody was a winner. They treated them all the same."

Roger looked at her incredulously. "That doesn't make any sense. How do you instill a sense of achievement if you teach them that everybody wins?"

"It's just how this generation was raised. But with that in mind, I have a suggestion."

"I'm open to any you can provide," Roger said, shaking his head in frustration.

"Another thing this generation is really big on is rewards, small rewards for doing a good job. My kids play all kinds of games online and they get virtual medals and coins for making it to another level. Sometimes they can redeem the rewards for additional play or for hints on getting to another level. But most of the time, it's just for that warm feeling of being rewarded for having done something right."

"You want me to create a reward?" Roger asked.

"Yes," replied Ann. "It doesn't have to be anything with significant value. We have our monthly newsletter, *The Stewart Cycle*. What if we had a section that recognized people for doing a good job? It could be the "High Fives of the Month," or something like that to recognize people for a job well done. It wouldn't be just for Phil. It could be for anyone in the company. I've heard things about Holly down in packaging. She does such a good job her name would be in there every other newsletter."

"So when would I give one to Phil?"

"If he does a good job putting together a timeline you give him one of these recognitions. When he does a good job on the budget, he gets another one," replied Ann.

Roger slanted his head back and said, "So let me get this straight. You want me to reward him for doing something he's supposed to do anyway?"

"In a sense. It's kind of a combination of reward and incentive. You give Mark and me bonuses at the end of the year. That's a way of rewarding us for what we should have been doing anyway right? But it's also an incentive to continue doing it. Think of this as a similar perk."

Roger shook his head. "It just seems to me that this generation seems to have a huge sense of entitlement."

"They do," Ann agreed. "Our generation of parents has generally focused so much on their self-esteem that maybe we went overboard. We taught them that no one is better than they are. Parents in our generation have done more to befriend them than to be their disciplinarians. As a result they not only have that sense of entitlement, but also have a high level of self-confidence. The benefit of that is that they want to contribute right out of the gate and they have the confidence to do it."

"They remind me of some of the rich kids I grew up with," Roger replied.

"They're a lot like those kids," Ann said. "They're not used to going without things. They want things right away. But there's one other thing that's very different about this generation, Roger."

"What's that?"

"They grew up with this technology," Ann answered. "They've never known a world without it. Think back to your grandparents' generation. Some of them had to get water from a well and if nature called it meant a trip outside. Maybe that's where that expression came from. By the time our generation came around we had inside plumbing; we couldn't fathom going to an outside toilet and hot and cold running water is just a part of life. To our grandparents these were amazing new technological advancements for society. Our generation on the other hand has always viewed it as an expectation. This is how kids who have grown up at the tail end of the twentieth century view the Internet and the myriad other things we call technology. You and I have seen the introduction of cell phones and the Internet and watched all of it evolve to the point it is today."

"Yes," Roger agreed. "We've seen amazing technological advances in just the last two decades."

"But that's the difference," Ann said. "Phil's generation doesn't see it as technology. To them, it's always been there. It's like running water to them."

Roger looked at Ann deep in thought. Finally he said, "That's a very interesting concept."

Ann continued, "As a result, they're very comfortable with the technology. You and I have apprehensions about any new technology. Their attitude is 'bring it on.' They're very open to changes and advances in all of this stuff. That's why he knows so much about social media and blogging. He's not just learning it, he uses it every day, as commonly as using the kitchen sink. So as much as you have to teach him and mentor him about business, he has some things he can teach all of us about the new technology."

Roger's head jerked back in a shocked realization. "It's amazing that you said that. Last week when we had our meeting where he introduced all of those ideas to change our website he made a smart-ass comment about giving me a 'mentoring moment.'"

Ann laughed out loud.

Roger continued, "I thought he was just being a cocky young kid. But based on what you've said today, he was probably serious. And worse yet... he was right." Roger looked down, shaking his head as he absorbed the reality.

Ann said nothing. Her hands were folded with her elbows on the arms of the chair. She smiled and nodded at Roger.

Roger's Journal

I don't know if I'll ever figure out this generation. There are times when Phil seems disrespectful and entitled. At other times he seems to know the technology that kids his age use. I should probably sit down and try to learn some of this from him, but I don't want to fuel his cocky attitude.

Chapter 12 – In Production

The morning sun shone in Roger's eyes as he pedaled down Randolph Street. On beautiful days like this he almost wished he lived further from the office so he could enjoy a longer bike ride. He arrived at the plant at the same time Phil pulled up on his bicycle.

"Good morning, Phil. Nice day to ride."

"It sure is," Phil replied. "I almost just kept going."

Roger laughed. "Me too, but I'm glad you stopped."

Roger took his helmet off and started walking in. Phil stayed with his bike, pulled out his smartphone, and started keying faster with two thumbs than Roger had seen some accomplished typists do with ten digits. He smiled, shook his head, and walked inside.

As the nine o'clock status meeting began, Ann and Mark were standing in Roger's office chatting when Phil entered. "This rounds out our crew," Roger said. "Let's get started. Phil, why don't you give us an update on your progress?"

Phil had already connected his laptop to the projector and had the company website exhibited on the wall. "As you can see, we have the link to my blog and our three initial social media icons on our main page. I won't go into each one, but if I click the Twitter button, it gives me the option to follow the Twitter handle for Stewart Bicycle Manufacturing, @StewartCycle." The rest of the team smiled and nodded.

"You'll also notice that a thumbnail for the first video is here on the page." Phil clicked the thumbnail, which began showing the video of Roger being interviewed. "Lori is still working on edits for the second video. We should have that loaded in the next week or so."

"This looks very nice Phil," Ann said. The others nodded in agreement.

"Thanks. With Mark's assistance, I've also been monitoring hits to the website. We've seen a two-hundred-percent increase in hits to the website and a five percent increase in online sales." The others broke out into applause at that news.

"One thing to keep in mind," Mark added, "is that this coincides with our increase in billboard advertising. We can't attribute it all to the online additions."

"That's true," Phil said, appearing to agree. "But the analytics show that a majority of the five percent increase is sourced from these online changes." Mark simply nodded.

"Regardless of where it comes from, it's great news to see these numbers," Roger added. "Do you have a report on your timeline and budget Phil?"

"I do," Phil replied.

Phil hot-keyed over to a spreadsheet that showed his timeline. "We're a little behind our original schedule. I had originally intended to be done by now. Lori is taking a little longer than planned to complete the second video. I also didn't expect the web development folks to take as long as they did."

"What is your new projection for completion?" Roger asked.

"Not sure," Phil responded rather nonchalantly. "It depends on when Lori finishes that video and how long it takes them to post it."

Roger wanted to say something but bit his lip. "How about the budget?"

Phil switched to another tab in the spreadsheet to display his budget. "As you can see, we're a bit over budget, too."

"A bit?" Roger asked. "You're at nearly a thousand dollars. I had only allocated five hundred."

"Well," said Phil, "I didn't realize how much it would cost for Web Page Solutions to do their work. And Lori is kind of a perfectionist. She's taken a lot more time to put these two videos together than I ever dreamed."

Roger counted to ten. Finally, he said, "Okay Phil, how much more time and money do you think it will take to complete this project?"

"It shouldn't be much more," Phil answered. "Lori will finish the video this weekend and then the web developers will post it. I hope we can have it all up by next week sometime. But I also wanted to look into adding a podcast."

"A what?" Roger asked. "No. Whatever that is, it needs to wait. Let's stick to the original plan. If they finish it all up by the end of next week, how much will it cost?"

"Probably about eleven hundred dollars," Phil replied.

"Okay," Roger said tersely. "We have our one-on-one scheduled after this meeting. We can talk in more detail about this then."

They moved on to other business. Ann reported that a delivery deadline for a new customer was missed. She added that the delivery would be about a week late and that she had personally spoken to the customer.

"Why was that order late?" Roger asked in an almost snippy response. "It looked like it was almost ready to ship this time last week. What was the holdup?"

Nobody spoke. Ann looked at Mark. Mark looked at Phil. "Well?" asked Roger. "Does anybody know why it's been going nowhere for the week?" Still the room was silent. "I shouldn't be surprised. Every time I turn around I see people tweeting and using their phones instead of working."

"We've kind of spread the word to everyone to share our blog and start sharing our web presence," Phil replied.

"Well what good does it do if we can't maintain a production schedule? If they want to do that kind of stuff they should do it on their own time." Roger was losing his patience. Again, there was a pregnant pause in the room. Finally, Roger spoke up. "Ann, what can we do to expedite this order to get it out sooner?"

"We've expanded the shifts and transferred some people from lower priority orders. We should be able to get this out without too much damage to the relationship," Ann said.

The rest of the meeting went swiftly. Everyone was interested in finishing up and getting out without prolonging the agony any further. When the meeting was adjourned, Phil stuck around to meet with Roger for their scheduled one-on-one meeting.

When Ann and Mark closed the door behind them, Roger spoke up. "I'm sorry I lost my temper a bit there, Phil. But believe it or not, I was holding back. You've projected to be more than a week past schedule and you've totally blown the budget I allocated to you. On top of that, this online stuff has had a negative effect on our plant productivity, which caused us to miss an important delivery deadline."

"But sales are up Roger." Phil said defensively.

"As nice as that is, it's beside the point. I'm trying to impress on you the importance of working toward a plan and tracking your project. You just can't keep meandering haphazardly without keeping things in check. You mentioned that sales are up a little. What if I ended up investing two thousand dollars in this and only get a thousand back in return? That's a negative return. It would be a bad investment."

Phil simply nodded in response.

"Can you push Lori to get this video done this weekend so that we can finish it up?" Roger asked.

'Yeah," said Phil, "we have a date tonight, so I'll talk to her then."

Roger's head jerked back in astonishment. "Wait a minute. Lori is your girlfriend?"

"Yeah. I thought you knew that."

Roger paused and wrung his hands waiting for the right words to come. "Phil, hiring your girlfriend is a conflict of interest."

"What do you mean?" Phil asked innocently.

"When you hire someone close to you like that, you don't have the same leverage you would normally have. You can't make independent decisions."

"She's the best video producer I know and she works for less than a full-fledged professional."

"Maybe," said Roger, "but what if she did a terrible job on the first video? How would you fire your girlfriend? Or what if you broke up during this project? Would she continue to work for you?"

"I hadn't thought of those things," Phil replied. "I mean, she did a good job on the first one and we're not breaking up. But I know what you mean."

Roger maintained his composure. "Phil, here's what I want you to do. Talk to Lori this weekend and try to get her to commit to finish editing the video by Monday. Talk to the web developers today and get them to schedule loading it to the website as soon as possible after they receive it from her. Starting Monday, I want to have a daily five-minute touch-base at nine o'clock sharp. In those meetings, I want you to give me the status of our progress on the timeline and budget. When Lori is done, get an invoice from her and I'll pay it. Do the same with the web developers. I want this finished by the end of next week."

Phil humbly nodded his head in agreement.

Phil's Evernote

The Reluctant Mentor

Roger sure blew up at me today. It seems even when I do what he asks me to do, he still isn't happy. Even when I created a timeline and budget like he asked, the information wasn't good enough for him. The work I'm doing has increased his bicycle sales and we haven't even scratched the surface. I'm beginning to think he can't be pleased. Some simple recognition would be nice.

Roger's journal

Phil is starting to show some progress. He's gotten most of the things done that I've asked for. He just doesn't seem to understand some business basics. I finally got him to create a budget, but he went more than one hundred percent over budget on it. He also hired his girlfriend for a job. After talking to him about that, I hope he sees that that's not a good idea. I'll keep working with him and get him in shape one of these days.

Chapter 13 – Trade Show

His rolling luggage got caught on three seats as he tried rolling it down the narrow aisle. When he finally got to his assigned seat, the overhead bin was full. Looking around him, he realized that the closest space to put his suitcase was three rows behind him. That will make getting off the plane a real breeze, Roger thought to himself sarcastically. Roger traveled for business once a year, for the annual sporting goods convention. As much as he enjoyed the convention and the chance to spend a few days in Chicago, he often wondered if it was worth the headaches of traveling to get there.

To Roger's delight, the flight went smoothly. A gentleman behind him on the plane handed his suitcase to him when they landed, saving him a few minutes disembarking. The cab ride was pleasant with very little traffic into the city. It gave Roger some time to think as he admired the beauty of the oncoming Chicago skyline. He began to wonder what he was going to do about Phil. I need to figure out a way to get across to him how important it is to follow a plan and stay on track, he thought to himself. When he began to get fidgety as they entered the loop, he decided to put Phil and technology out of his mind for the week. He was going to enjoy his time at the trade show.

Roger checked into his hotel and put his luggage in his room. He took a look around to make sure everything was in order. Opening the curtains, he saw a beautiful view of Lake Michigan. "Now this is how to live," he said out loud.

After admiring the view for a moment, he grabbed his room key from the table and headed for the elevators. He knew some of the friends he had made on previous trips made a habit a congregating in the hotel bar the night before the show began. This year was no different. As soon as he walked in he recognized two gentlemen he had known for years.

He made eye contact with Jim Vandercook first. Jim owned a boating supplies manufacturing company based in Milwaukee. Roger met Jim nine years earlier at this very trade show. He purchased his first fishing boat soon after and Jim sent him a "boat-warming" gift that included life jackets, specialized tackle, and some nylon anchor line. Roger returned the favor by sending him one of his latest models of bicycles. A friendship was formed and they always enjoyed spending time together during trade-show week.

Jim was talking to Mike Curran, a mutual friend to Roger and Jim. Mike owned a small chain of ski shops in the Denver area. Mike enjoyed outdoors sports the same as Roger and they had spent many hours in previous trade shows one-upping each other in a friendly manner with their various outdoor adventures.

After saying their hellos, Jim told Roger that he and Mike had been discussing how they were using technology to sell their products. Roger resisted the urge to roll his eyes, having just vowed to put that out of his mind for the week.

"I'm a local shop that sells mainly to people in my area," said Mike. "Most of my online presence is about making people aware of our stores and what we sell. Then I want to help them find the closest store. I don't sell anything online."

"I sell some products online," Jim interjected. "But I try to be careful not to compete with the retailers I sell to. I don't want to undercut them in any way. But we have a presence on the major social media sites and are always trying to improve our SEO."

Esseo? Roger thought. He made a mental note to find out what that was. He didn't want to embarrass himself by asking his peers. He did tell the boys the efforts that Phil was implementing and they showed some interest. Fortunately, the conversation drifted to other topics and Roger was able to ease his mind a bit. He cut out early to get a good night's sleep for the first day of the show.

The convention was set in McCormick Place on Chicago's lakeshore. Every year Roger marveled at the size of the facilities and the number of people that must go through it every year. After twenty minutes of standing in line and getting registered, he proceeded to the main hall. He had pre-registered for a few seminars, but his main objective, the activities he enjoyed most, was walking from booth to booth meeting with the various vendors. He liked seeing what his competition was up to. Not just bicycle manufacturers; he checked out all the sporting goods manufacturers. If someone was doing something for fun outdoors, whether it be fishing or playing volleyball, he saw that as a potential competitor, pulling people away from biking.

He stopped at the booth of a skateboard manufacturer. Their display included a large skateboarding ramp with professional skateboarders doing loops and tricks with their skateboards. While the gathered crowd was mesmerized by the skateboarders, Roger struck up a conversation with the man who seemed to be in charge of the booth. He was a young man who Roger figured was about Phil's age.

Roger introduced himself and explained his business to the young man.

"I'm Ryan Paul. I started making skateboards in our garage when I was in high school."

"That's interesting." Roger said. "That's how I started making bicycles. I wasn't in high school, but it just started in the garage. How did you move from garage to full-scale manufacturing?"

"My dad saw how successful it had become and invested in me. He and I are business partners now," said Ryan.

After learning more than he wanted about how successful Ryan had become at such a young age, Roger decided to see if he did any of the things Phil had been introducing.

"Do you sell many of you skateboards online?" Roger asked.

"There are a few stores near us in California that sell traditional retail. But we sell about ninety-five percent online," answered Ryan.

"Interesting. What tactics do you use to draw people to your site?"

"We use a lot of SEO tactics. We blog and post a lot of videos of people using our boards. We're on all the social media sites. How about you?"

"We have a blog on biking and a couple of videos. And we're on a few social media sites," Roger answered proudly, feeling he was running with the big dogs with his tech talk. He sensed just a hint of Ryan being impressed with the old guy being able to hold such a conversation. This guy just brought up "esseo" again, Roger thought to himself. He made another mental note to find out what that term meant. Still, he was glad he was doing the same things this young guy was doing. He also realized how much Phil had taught him in such a short time. Three months ago, he wouldn't have been able to go toe-to-toe with a young hot shot like that.

When Friday rolled around, Roger was ready to head back to Roanoke. He had had a fun week, learned a lot, and was taking a lot of new ideas home with him. But he was ready to go home. One week in Chicago was enough to remind him that Roanoke was his home.

After a jaunt through O'Hare International Airport that seemed like a leg from a triathlon, he got to gate C15 to find out his flight had been delayed. Here we go, he thought. He sat down in the gate area and looked around. There weren't very many people. He wondered if they were going to cancel the flight.

"How long do you think we'll be stuck here?" Roger looked to his right and saw a young man two seats down from him.

"I don't know," Roger replied with a smile. "I'm not too keen on sleeping in the terminal though."

The man smiled and extended his hand. "I'm Chad Harrison."

"Nice to meet you, Chad. I'm Roger, Roger Stewart."

"Are you from Chicago or just visiting and heading home?"

The Reluctant Mentor

Roger told Chad about the sporting goods convention and his bicycle manufacturing business. Chad asked several questions about how he got started and built his business up from scratch. Roger always enjoyed talking about his business and appreciated anyone who took an interest in hearing his story.

Roger enjoyed talking with Chad so much that there was a slight look of disappointment on his face when the announcement came on that they would be boarding. "Well, I guess that's us," he said to Chad.

"Yes, what's your seat assignment?" Chad asked.

"8B," Roger said, looking at his ticket.

"I'm a little further back, but it doesn't look like a full plane at all. Perhaps I could sit across the isle from you and we could continue our conversation."

"I'd enjoy that," Roger said.

Once on the plane and settled in, Roger turned to Chad and asked what brought him to Chicago.

"I've been visiting a client. I own an IT business. We started out developing applications mainly for small businesses. We still do that, but we began focusing on smartphone apps."

Roger looked at him and guessed he couldn't be a day over twenty-eight. He was intrigued that a man so young was the head of his own software company.   "How did you get your start?" he quizzed.

"When I first got out of college, I started working as a software developer for a large insurance company. My manager was a guy named Bruce who had several years more experience than me. He kind of took me under his wing. He would give me advice about managing different situations. We would meet for lunch and he would talk about different matters he had experienced in his career, how he had messed up and what he would do differently now. One day he told me about a friend who owned a small business and needed some help. I started working evenings and weekends to develop software for him. Before I knew it, this guy had referred me to some other people and I had a budding business."

"That's incredible. How long did you do both jobs?"

"It was almost a year," Chad replied. "Once I made enough to pay my bills with my side job, I quit the insurance company and went entirely independent. I eventually hired some employees and we've been growing ever since."

"It sounds like Bruce was a big influence in your career," Roger said.

"I didn't realize it at the time. I thought Bruce and I were just talking. But he was intentionally setting me on a path for success and so many of the little lessons and advice he gave me still apply for me today. We're still good friends and meet for lunch once in a while. I just met with him last week and told him what an influence he had been on my career. He confided in me that he also learned a lot from me. He told me that I had introduced him to a lot of new technologies that he hadn't even been aware of. I didn't realize it, but we were both kind of mentoring each other."

"That's very interesting," said Roger.

"Another important thing he did for me was encouragement to get out and talk to others about business and career--to network. I remember him saying to me, 'Don't just accept my advice, check it out with others.'"

"So how did you do that?" inquired Roger.

"He was a member of the local Chamber of Commerce and they had weekly business briefings. I was allowed to leave work early on Thursdays to go to these events where all kinds of people would gather to listen to a speaker for a short talk. The rest of the time was meeting new people."

Chad continued, "At first I felt out of place, but the more I got to know the people there, the easier it got. I made a bunch of contacts that I still talk to today. It also taught me how to meet people in person. It's easy to meet people online, but going up and talking to someone in person can be a little scary. I still try to get to a networking event at least a couple of times a month, and not with the same group each time."

The Reluctant Mentor

"That's true," Roger agreed, thinking of his own regular networking at the Roanoke Business Owners lunches and making a silent promise to himself to mix more at future events.

"Our mentoring relationship continues to this day," Chad said. "We still confide in each other and seek advice about various things. It's turned out to be the most influential relationship I've had in my career."

When the plane landed the two men shook hands and exchanged business cards. Roger realized that, despite the delay in Chicago, it was one of the most pleasant business travel experiences he had ever had. He was impressed with Chad starting his business and becoming so successful at such a young age. Chad was lucky to have met someone like Bruce who saw the potential in him and began helping him develop so early in his career.

On his drive home from the airport, it occurred to Roger that that was the type of relationship he had with Phil. Roger realized that he had a responsibility to Phil. As his boss and mentor, he is affecting Phil's life direction. Roger saw the same entrepreneurial spirit in Phil and realized that Phil may have as much to teach him as he could teach Phil.

I'm going to have a little talk with Phil tomorrow when I'm back, he said to himself.

The Reluctant Mentor

The next day Ann walked up to Phil in the hallway. "Hi, Phil. I was just talking to Roger in his office. He's back from the trade show and wanted to talk to you."

"Thanks, Ann." Phil was hoping to get some time with Roger. He wanted to hear all about the trade show.

Roger saw him as soon as he stuck his head in the door. "Come on in, Phil," he said jubilantly.

Phil sat down and asked, "How was your trip?"

Roger told him about the trade show and some of the new trends he had seen in the bicycling industry. He also explained what he learned from alternative sports like skateboarding, which had potential to cut into their market. But he saved his most valuable lesson from the trade show for last.

"Listen Phil, I've been talking to you about these 'mentoring moments,' where I've given you advice on kind of an as-needed basis."

Phil nodded, a bit confused at Roger's change in direction.

Roger continued, "Rather than have these informal mentoring moments, I'd like to set up a standing one-hour weekly meeting for us to mentor. But these sessions will have a twist. The first half will be me mentoring you on the importance of things like planning, metrics, accountability, considering direct and indirect costs, and so forth."

Phil nodded without expression.

"The other half," Roger continued, "will be you mentoring me."

Phil slanted his head to one side a bit more confused now.

"Remember the other day when you kind of joked about a 'mentoring moment' for me? I've really taken that to heart. After thinking about it, I realized that you had a point. I also realized in some of my conversations at the trade show how much you've already taught me about using newer technologies for marketing. I think these approaches can have some significant value and I'd like to learn more," Roger said.

Phil smiled and said, "That sounds like a great idea. When can we start?"

Roger's journal

My trip to Chicago for the trade show was successful. As always, I learned a lot about what is going on in the industry and it was nice to see some old friends. But I think the most educational part of the trip was meeting Chad on the way home. He opened my eyes to the fact that I can learn as much from Phil as he can learn from me. I think my pride was in the way and was stuck on the idea that this mentoring thing could only go one way--down.

Chad also made me think about networking and that maybe I should encourage Phil to get involved with some of the general networking events that the Roanoke Business Owners hold on the last Thursday of the month.

Phil's Evernote

I don't know what happened to Roger in Chicago, but I sure am glad he went. I knew he would get some new ideas from the trade show. But his biggest idea was for us to mentor each other. I knew he wanted to mentor me and there is probably a lot I can learn from him. But he also wants me to mentor him. I never really realized I was the mentoring type, let alone with someone with that much more experience. I'm looking forward to our first session.

Chapter 14 – Bidirectional Mentoring Is Good

In their first formal mentoring meeting Roger spent about twenty minutes explaining to Phil some of the business concepts that he attributed to his success. He discussed the benefits of planning and how he had learned to develop production schedules when he opened his first legitimate plant. Phil confidently pushed back, asking what Roger did when factors changed causing his future plans to take a different route.

"That happens on a nearly daily basis," Roger explained. "As you've probably seen, we make frequent adjustments. That's just the nature of business."

He went on to show Phil some of his financial controls, his annual budget, and the company's balance sheet. Phil had had some exposure to some of these documents in textbooks in college, but had not seen them in actual use.

"I'll admit that some of this is as boring as a subtitled movie," Roger conceded. "But these metrics are the necessary evils we have to create to make sure we're financially sound, or, to find out if we're not."

The Reluctant Mentor

"Metrics?" Phil asked. "Isn't that the measuring system they use in Europe?"

Roger chuckled. "Good point, yes it is but a metric is also a term we use for any business measurements. You see, even conversations like this teach us things. You have learned a new business term, and I'm reminded not to assume that your audience understands the terms you are using."

Phil nodded, taking it all in. He agreed that the accounting was boring, but it helped him to realize that there was more to running a business than just going to meetings.

"Next week, I'd like to talk to you about how Ann, Mark, and I strategize on an annual and quarterly basis. But I'd like to get to your part of the meeting. I got a number of ideas from the companies I met at the trade show last week. I've been studying some of the websites of these companies and I've come to the conclusion that our website is a bit out of date. I like the tweaks you made to our site. I think they're a good temporary solution to our old site. But I'd like to totally redo the site. It looks old and tired. We aren't using e-commerce appropriately. It just doesn't have that sexy look that some of these other firms seem to have."

Phil raised his eyebrows at Roger. "What research have you done to make you so certain we should make this big jump? Have you considered the return on investment of such an undertaking? What will your marketing strategy be for this project?"

Roger wasn't sure what to say at first. Then he saw the smirk on Phil's face as they both broke into laugher. "You have learned well, Grasshopper."

Before long, they were deep in discussion. Roger admitted that he had only heard the concept of e-commerce at the trade show. Phil explained to Roger how a true e-commerce site would allow them to streamline their online order processing. Roger asked Phil what "esseo" is and Phil went on a fifteen-minute monologue explaining that S-E-O stands for Search Engine Optimization. It is a way to make your website compatible with search engines so that your content can be more easily located by people searching for your products and services. He went on more about the competitiveness of obtaining high rankings on the search engines, how the rules are constantly changed by those search engines, and how adding the blog, social media links, and videos had improved their SEO over the past couple of months.

Roger listened closely, thanking his lucky stars that he hadn't embarrassed himself by spelling the acronym as a word. He was intrigued with the amount of information that Phil knew about these new technologies. He had a list of topics he had written down from the trade show and had only scratched the surface. He was looking forward to their next session.

The Reluctant Mentor

"Before you go Phil," Roger said, "there's one more thing."

"Uh-oh," Phil uttered nervously, wondering what was coming.

"This is optional, but highly recommended," Roger said. "I'd like to encourage you to attend some business networking events. Don't take the advice that I give you as gospel, talk it over with others as you get the chance. And the best way to do that is to network with other business people."

"How am I going to do that?" Phil asked. "I guess I could connect with more people on LinkedIn?"

"You missed the point, Phil. This is about face-to-face networking--meeting and talking. "It's a low-tech novel concept," Roger said sarcastically with a smile.

"Very funny," Phil responded, "but where can I network around here?" he asked.

"You know I belong to the Roanoke Business Owners Network?" Roger asked, but continued before getting a response from Phil. "Well they hold an after-work gathering on the last Thursday of the month that anyone can attend. It only costs about twenty dollars and you get to hear someone talk about some aspect of business, share a couple of drinks, and meet some interesting people. I thought I'd bring you along to the next event and introduce you around. After that it's up to you."

The Reluctant Mentor

"Okay," Phil said hesitantly. "I'm not convinced I will get anything more out of it compared to hooking up on LinkedIn but you are the mentor."

"And so are you Phil," Roger quipped. "Maybe you can even convince me to take a closer look at LinkedIn."

The next day at the Roanoke Business Owners Networking meeting, Roger was anxious to talk to his colleagues. Robb and Jon were happy to see their friend. "We missed you last week Roger," Robb said. "How was the trade show?"

"It was very informative, but that's just the half of it. You guys won't believe everything that's gone down in the last couple of weeks." Roger went on to explain his conversations with Ann at lunch and with Chad on the plane home. He described the realization that, as much as he felt he had to teach Phil, Phil had a lot to teach him in return. When he told Robb and Jon about the mentoring sessions he had set up with Phil, they looked at him like he had three arms.

"Let me get this straight. You've set up sessions for Phil to mentor you?" Jon asked.

Roger nodded his head and laughed. "As soon as I swallowed my pride and realized that I didn't know everything, I realized that this young buck had a few things he could teach me. I may have learned more in that session from him than he learned from me."

"Like what?" Robb asked, his interest piqued.

Roger explained the discussion he had with Phil on e-commerce, which validated what he had seen on the websites of a majority of the tradeshow's attendees. He told them about search engine optimization and how "Google-juice" was the Holy Grail for getting people to their websites.

Jon shook his head. "That may be well and good for you. You sell bikes online. I don't see myself selling baked goods over the Internet."

"Perhaps," Roger replied. "But you could still benefit by having a website that ranks high for the search engines. What if someone in the area is looking for a bakery nearby?"

"They can just go to the Yellow Pages," Jon replied.

"They can. But they probably won't. The people who do that are a dying breed," Roger explained. "They're more likely to go to a search engine like Google or Bing and search for bakeries in the area. If your competitors come up first, that's where they're more likely to go."

Jon had no response to that, but it prompted Robb to join in. "So this stuff isn't just for selling online, it's to get more people to our store?"

"It all boils down to basic marketing," Roger explained. "They're new tools, but all of this makes people more aware of your presence. It may bring them into your store or it might just remind them of your brand for the next time they need something."

"I wish I had a Phil at my company that I could bounce ideas off of," responded Robb. "I wouldn't mind having someone look at my website to give me some ideas."

"You both probably have a few Phils lurking around your store," Roger replied. "You should just sit down with some of these folks. A lot of them have websites and blogs of their own. They're constantly experimenting with this stuff."

"I'll start some conversations," Robb said. "I may have some untapped knowledge right under my nose."

"Maybe I'll ask around, too," Jon said. "Some of your points make a lot of sense."

"I have an idea," Roger inserted. "What if each of us identifies one person in our organization that has some familiarity with these technologies? We could have a summit between our three companies. Each of us with our younger counterparts could discuss different ideas and how they could apply for each of our different businesses."

"That's a great idea." Robb said.

Jon finally spoke up, "I don't know which I like better, your idea for collaboration or the Italian food."

"I call it a tie," said Robb as he loaded some more tortellini on his plate.

Phil's Evernote

The Reluctant Mentor

Roger and I had a great session. He has explained aspects of the business that I never knew existed. There is a lot of paperwork and number crunching that goes on behind the scenes. I had some exposure to a lot of these tools from some of my business classes, but had never seen how it all falls together. I'm looking forward to next week's session where he'll talk to me about how they develop strategy. It sounds interesting.

He's also suddenly very excited about improving our web presence. This trade show must have really opened his eyes to what other companies are doing. He's asking some great questions.

Roger's Journal

I had a great session with Phil today. He seems genuinely interested in the business approaches, even with accounting procedures that I figured would bore him silly. He also knows a lot about helping us get a more modern website that will allow us to process orders better and get more business. I think even Robb and Jon are coming around to see the benefits of this.

Chapter 15 – Next Level Deeper

Roger smiled at Phil. "I've been looking forward to this meeting all week," he said as Phil settled down in his office.

"Me too," Phil said. "I've actually been reading up on strategy and how you develop a plan of attack."

"That's great." Roger said. He handed Phil the latest strategic plan that the executive team had developed. He explained to Phil how they put together a new strategic plan at the beginning of each year, readdressing it on a quarterly basis. Roger could tell that Phil had done his homework based on the questions he asked. Roger went on to describe how the team tracks their actual progress to their strategic plan and how they make adjustments when factors outside of their control send them down a new direction.

After about thirty minutes of strategy chat, Roger said, "That's my session for the week. Let's move on to yours."

Roger picked up his small notebook and started thumbing through it, perusing the many pages of handwritten notes.

"What's that?" Phil asked.

The Reluctant Mentor

"This is just a personal journal that I keep. I make notes and lists and reminders to ask someone something, that sort of thing."

"I do the same thing," Phil said, "although you might remember me telling you that I use an online tool called Evernote. It allows me to search for things and categorize them so they're easy to find."

"Of course you do," said Roger, completely unsurprised at the difference in their approaches.

"So, how do you search for specific notes?" asked Phil.

"That's what I'm doing now. I wrote down some notes that I wanted to share with you. I'll find them in just a minute," Roger replied.

"Have you ever considered keeping your notes electronically?" Phil shot back. "You can search for keywords that you know are in the text and it finds them immediately. You can even store things in different categories to keep similar notes together."

"Let me make a note of that," Roger said sarcastically, pretending to write in his journal.

Phil knew Roger's sarcasm was directed more at himself than at Phil, so he let it go. "You know what we could do is start a wiki."

"A what?" asked Roger with a crinkled brow.

"A wiki. It's an online collaboration tool that allows multiple people to capture and share ideas."

Roger closed his journal and smiled. "Okay, topic one on our agenda is 'What are wikis?'."

Phil spent the next five minutes explaining how wikis work and how he could envision using one at their organization. Roger didn't fully grasp the usability of the tool, but was open-minded enough to give it a try. He could see where it was more beneficial than using endless e-mail threads for collaboration.

When Phil felt Roger understood the concept of wikis he had another topic in mind to discuss. "Are you familiar with podcasts?" he asked Roger.

"I've heard of them. There was a lot of talk of them in Chicago."

"Well, I was thinking that would be another thing to add to our online repertoire. A podcast is simply a recording--sort of a short radio show--that you post on your website and iTunes and other places where people can download it and listen to it whenever they want." Phil pulled out his smartphone and showed Roger his podcast app. "I download podcasts on all types of topics. Then I listen to them while I'm riding my bike, driving, or working out, pretty much whenever I'm alone."

Roger had several questions about how and where the podcasts would be recorded, who would record them, what content they would discuss and a number of other logistical matters. More importantly, it was such a foreign concept to him that Roger was confused about the value. He wanted to know who listened to podcasts. Was it worth the effort if only a few outliers downloaded and listened to them?

Phil patiently answered every one of his questions. He showed Roger some of the more popular podcasts on iTunes and their download statistics. When he showed Roger the statistics from companies in the sporting goods industry, he seemed to sit up and take notice.

Phil was as good of a student as he was a teacher. He applied the lessons he learned from Roger about the organization's long-term strategy and cost-justification. When he showed Roger the potential benefits of providing content to their market compared to the relatively low cost, Roger warmed to the idea.

"This is just one of several initiatives that we need to consider," Roger finally said. "I met a young gentleman on my flight home from Chicago that I'd like to bring in to work with us. His company does web development and I think they could work with us to develop a whole new website and help us get to where we need to go."

"That sounds great," said Phil. "When can he be here?"

Phil's Evernote

Roger amazes me more and more every day. He's already got a company in mind to help us develop a more modern website. I was worried that these mentoring sessions would be a drag but he's sharing some really interesting information with me. It's kind of fun teaching him a few things, too. Particularly things that will help take this company in another direction.

Roger's Journal

When I originally thought about mentoring Phil, I saw myself as a teacher. I have to admit that it was kind of an ego trip taking a fledgling rookie under my wing and shaping him into a man. But in our sessions, I find myself trying to get through my lesson so that I can learn from him. I don't look at him as the cocky young wise guy anymore. I see him as a knowledgeable person. We have complementary knowledge bases and are making progress sharing them with each other.

Chapter 16 – Chad's Approach

Roger introduced Chad to Phil, Mark, and Ann and they all sat down in his office to discuss the new website for Stewart Bicycle Manufacturing. Roger explained his interest in making this a team effort that would incorporate a holistic market view for how they would reach customers across their market spectrum.

Over the next several weeks the team of five, along with occasional specialists from Chad's company, met to discuss, plan, and design how the new website should look, what they would communicate to their market, and how they would regularly update their content to ensure effective search engine optimization. Roger marveled at how the words that once seemed to be "buzz words" had turned into common terminology.

With most of the planning complete, they were ready to begin implementation. Chad suggested an iterative approach, developing small components at a time. Roger wasn't completely comfortable with the approach, but deferred to Chad's expertise.

The Reluctant Mentor

The first phase of the project was to develop the landing page, the initial page that most users would land on upon entering the website. Chad stated that this was critical because it was the first impression their users would have with the company. He worked with Phil and his own web designers to create what they called the "user experience." Over the course of a few weeks, they worked as a team designing, developing, redesigning, and redeveloping. Finally, Chad called a meeting with Roger and his team to give a showcase of the landing page.

Chad demonstrated the landing page, projecting it on the wall from his laptop. He explained the positioning of each item on the screen and the strategy behind each one's placement. He described where the various links would take the user once they were developed. The group seemed pleased with the progress they had made.

"I have a suggestion," Phil added when the demo was done. "You have those social media links at the bottom of the page. I think they should be at the top of the page as well. In fact, that should be the standard on all of the pages."

"That's a good idea," Chad responded. He made a note of Phil's suggestion and asked if anyone else had any questions.

"It looks very nice," Roger finally spoke up. "Do you have a timeline for finishing the rest of the site?"

"Not a full timeline per se," responded Chad. "My next agenda item was to determine with this team which component we should develop next and go from there."

Roger frowned. "I was hoping we would have a more comprehensive plan for implementation. Do you have an idea for when the whole website will be completed?"

"If I had to guess, it should take another month to six weeks to have a basic site up. We'll continue to build on it from there, but it really depends on what kind of issues come up and what we decide to ultimately do with each component."

Roger was frustrated with Chad's answer but held his tongue. He didn't want to get into a heated debate in front of the entire team. He decided he would talk to Chad privately. As the meeting drew to a close, Chad mentioned that he needed to run for another client meeting he had later that morning. Roger made a note to schedule some time to talk with Chad.

The team filed out of Roger's office. Mark stayed behind and closed Roger's door when the last person walked out. "Do you have a minute, Roger?"

"Sure."

"I sensed some frustration on your face dealing with Chad's approach."

Roger smiled and shook his head. "Did I make it that obvious?"

Mark returned a smile. "I don't think anyone else noticed, but I've known you for a long time."

"It just seems to be that generation's approach of 'let's do it and see what happens.' I would just like them to spend more time on analysis. Figure out what you're going to do and then do it. They just want to jump in doing things a little at a time."

"Well, it is sort of their approach, but it's not as haphazard as it may seem. This is sort of an agile approach. They design and develop components in small sprints. Then they review what they have and decide on the next step. This gives them flexibility to make changes as they go. Remember when Web Page Solutions did our old website? We planned and designed the whole thing up front."

"Exactly," Roger replied, as if Mark was making his point for him.

"And then when all the design was complete," Mark continued, "they went off and developed the whole thing."

Roger nodded, waiting for Mark to get to the point.

"Do you remember the day they showed up here with the finished product? We liked most of what they did, but there were a couple of things they completely misinterpreted from our requirements."

Roger sat there nodding with his hands folded, looking up, as if the memory was being replayed on the ceiling.

Mark continued, "And there were some new things we thought of that didn't even come up until they showed us their completed work."

Roger nodded, still looking up, "If I remember correctly, we wanted to add some links or move them to a different page."

"Yeah, remember what a pain it was to make those changes? We had to pay them extra for the modifications and it delayed our ability to go live by about a month if I remember right. Chad's approach may be hard to follow because you don't see a full plan, but it should help avoid the problems we had the last time."

"How so?" Roger asked.

"Those changes Phil came up with during today's showcase? If Chad were doing this the way we did it before, we wouldn't have seen the need for them until the end of the project. Then they would have had to go back and change every page. This way, Chad can make the change immediately and implement the change on the remaining pages as they go. It just gives them more visibility into what we need and a lot more flexibility to change on the fly," Mark explained.

Roger slowly bobbed his head from side to side contemplating what Mark was telling him. "I do see the value of seeing the progress at various milestones. I would just feel better having a plan in my hand telling me when the project will be finished and whether we're on track."

"That's the trade-off of this agile approach," Mark said. "What you lose in certainty, you gain in flexibility. Give it a few more weeks and a couple of showcases and see what they come up with."

"Thanks, Mark, I will. And thanks for talking me off the ledge. I was pretty frustrated after that meeting."

"Just part of my job," Mark replied with a smile.

Roger's journal

I'm learning that the younger generation is not as aimless as I thought. Their approaches are less planned but intended for better flexibility to make changes. Once again, they're teaching this old dog some new tricks. I've swallowed more pride in the last few weeks than I have in a long time. And I'm learning more than I have in a long time. It seems to me that there may be a correlation.

Chapter 17 – Shake Up

Roger looked around the table at Amigoni's Ristorante. His faithful team of Mark, Ann, and Phil sat there with smiles as wide as his own. Additionally, Chad and three of his key team members rounded out the celebratory dinner.

Roger ordered a bottle of champagne for the table. When everyone's glass had been poured, he clinked his fork to his glass for attention.

"Ann, I think he wants us to kiss," joked Phil.

Roger shook his head and laughed but withheld comment. "I want to thank each and every one of you tonight. Tomorrow, we go live with the new website for Stewart Bicycle Manufacturing. Throughout this whole process, you may not have noticed, but I wasn't exactly on board with every idea."

Everyone at the table shared a joyful laugh as Roger joked at his own expense.

Roger continued, "But each of you has shown patience and perseverance. We've learned a lot in this process and I don't think anyone has learned as much as I have. It's been a great opportunity for me and I'm excited about the opportunities this new site will open up for our company." He held up his glass and said, "Here's to each and every one of you. Thank you."

Ann sensed a slight crack in his voice as he finished his sentence. She, along with the rest of them, raised her glass toward Roger and in unison, everyone said, "Cheers!"

The rest of the night was filled with joking and laughter as the team basked in the glory of their accomplishment. Phil sat and reflected on some of the early conversations he had with Roger and the team, the frustrations he had with their reluctance to try new ideas and how far they had all come since then. As excited as he was about how far they had come, he was even more excited about where they were going.

When dinner was over and the champagne was gone, Roger paid the bill and thanked everyone one last time. Each attendee returned the thank you to Roger and began preparing to leave. Mark lingered around. When everyone else had left the restaurant, he asked Roger if he would join him for a drink in the bar. Roger could tell that more than just a drink was involved and complied.

With a shot of Amaretto in front of each of them, Roger turned to Mark. "So what's up?"

The Reluctant Mentor

Mark looked Roger straight in the eye. "Roger, I've been with you for over fifteen years. We've been through a lot together."

"We sure have. Has it been that long?"

"I agree that it's gone quick. Roger, let me get to the point. You know about my interest in classic cars, right?"

"Sure," said Roger. "You've refurbished some beauties."

"Don Cooper from Cooper's Classic Cars called me last week. He's looking for someone to head up his marketing department."

Roger smiled and bowed his head. When he raised it back up he showed two fingers to the bartender indicating the need for another round. Finally, he looked back at Mark. "This is your dream job isn't it?"

"Yes. Believe me, I wasn't looking. He just approached me out of the blue."

Roger put his hand on Mark's shoulder. "I understand Mark. This is a great opportunity for you. I'd never begrudge you something like this."

"Thanks, Roger," Mark said with some relief in his voice.

"But you might want to warn Don that this is going to cost him a couple of cases of wine."

They both laughed and raised their glasses in a toast.

"As happy as I am for you," Roger added, "I still have to figure out how I'm going to replace you."

Mark raised his eyebrows, "Really? I think the answer is as clear as the nose on your face."

Roger studied Mark's face. "Phil?"

"Roger, he may not have an MBA in marketing, but he knows his stuff. Most of the marketing we have in place was based on his ideas. With that and the mentoring you've done with him, I think he's the logical person to take on this role."

"I suppose. He just seems so young," Roger said, mulling it over.

"He's only a few years younger than I was when I started," Mark coaxed.

"I'll think about it," Roger replied. "How long do I have you for?"

"I told Don I'd need at least two weeks. If you need more, we can probably work something out."

Roger finished his drink and stood up. "This is a decision I'd like Ann's input on. I'll touch base with her in the morning and follow up with you after that." He put his right hand toward Mark. "Congratulations, my boy, my loss is Don Cooper's gain."

Mark shook his hand and thanked his boss and friend.

Roger's journal

The Reluctant Mentor

Just when I thought we were running on all pistons, Mark threw a monkey wrench in the works. His leaving the company was not in my plans. I do think that the challenge of replacing him can bring about some opportunities. I was actually worried more about losing Phil. This gives me the chance to promote Phil and have better odds of keeping him on board. I'm sure he'll do fine as the company's new marketing director.

Chapter 18 – Technology Never Stops

Phil laughed out loud giving Lori a start. "What are you laughing at?" she called from the kitchen.

"Roger just friended me on Facebook," Phil said.

She stuck her head in the room. "Your boss, Roger?"

"Yeah. Four months ago he probably thought Facebook was where the police kept their mug shots. Now he's friending me."

"Are you going to accept?"

"Sure," said Phil. "He's come a long way. He's been commenting on my blogs and even writing guest blogs. He told me the other day that he finally got on LinkedIn and found out that most of his tradeshow friends were already on it."

"It sounds like you've taught him quite a bit," she said with some pride.

"It's been a two way street," he replied. "I've got to get to work," he added, giving her a kiss goodbye.

When he arrived at work it was still strange for him to walk down the management corridor to Mark's old office.

After nearly three weeks he had settled in a bit, but it still felt strange.

As Phil sat down, Roger stuck his head in his door. "Have you seen the website numbers yet?"

"No, I was just logging in," Phil replied.

"Since we went live with the new site, sales are up twenty percent," Roger said in an almost giddy voice.

"That's terrific," Phil said with a smile.

Roger grabbed a chair and sat down across from Phil's desk. "We've made a lot of progress over the past few months. It was fairly tumultuous at times, but we made it through."

"You were a trouper," Phil said with a smile.

"I couldn't have done it without you, Phil. You were an injection of energy and new ideas when the company needed it. I'm glad to see things settling down a bit."

Phil stood up and walked to the whiteboard in his office. "Let's not settle down too much," he said, pointing to a list on the whiteboard. "I've got more plans. I was thinking of developing a mobile app. There are a lot of ideas I have for that. I also think we could implement an e-mail list for a monthly newsletter. Some of the other ideas I want to talk about …"

The Reluctant Mentor

As Phil continued down the list, Roger saw the number of ideas Phil had on his whiteboard. He felt his eyes roll to the back of his head. Will it never end? he asked himself.

"Before you go, Roger," Phil asked, "are you going to the Tavern tonight? I'm speaking at the IT HotSpot networking event about Blogging for Business. It might be good for you to get out there and network a bit. You might meet some interesting people"

Roger replied with a knowing smirk. "Thanks for the tip, Phil. I'll see you there. It must be your turn to buy drinks."

Roger's Evernote

I was working with Phil today on a few items and was suddenly struck by how much he has taught me about the positive use of technology in our business, despite my early resistance. Our joint mentoring relationship hasn't been very formal, just an organic and natural respect for each other and an openness that has given us both the opportunity to learn, teach, challenge, and explore in ways that I've never experienced with peers of my own generation. I must take the time to talk to him about this and thank him in some way.

I'm also amazed at how much he has changed in such a short period. He has grown from a college grad to a competent and driven businessperson since working with us. I'd like to think I had something to do with this but I see the same fire in his belly I had at his age and he would probably have excelled at anything he put his mind to.

For the first time, I'm wondering if our little company can keep him motivated. I can see that he has the capability to do more and I hope we can provide enough challenge and excitement for him but it wouldn't surprise me if he decides to move on at some point, either to another company or to start his own business. I need to consider this as a possibility and have a game plan in preparation.

As I think about this possibility, I feel somewhat conflicted. I've helped him grow and the company has also grown along with us, what will happen if he leaves suddenly? But I can't overlook the positive changes he has made in me, all as a result of a few mentoring moments.

Epilogue

The traditional approach to mentoring--whether it was done formally or informally--was for the older and wiser workers to mentor the younger, greener workers, handing their experience down to the next generation.

This is a sensible approach and one that many people today still accept. However, Generation Y is much more unique than their preceding generations. This generation, born roughly between the early 1980s and early 2000s, has some very unique characteristics. They have grown up with technology. Most of them do not remember a world without the Internet or mobile phones. Additionally, the majority of their parents raised them in an environment where there were no losers--everyone got a trophy. As they grew into young adults, they viewed their parents as friends and collaborators rather than authority figures or disciplinarians.

As a result, members of Generation Y are unique from two major perspectives:

Technology has always been around them. They know it intimately and are exceedingly comfortable with it. When new advances in technology are introduced they embrace it, where older generations tend to be more skeptical or even afraid. It can be argued that they don't view "technology" as anything unique, it's just inherently a part of their life, like running water and electricity.

They feel a sense of self-credibility. As they enter the business world, they want to contribute immediately. The baby boomer generation (people born post–World War II to the 1960s) may interpret this as a sense of entitlement. They expect the Generation Yers to "know their place," respect their elders, and allow the older generation to "show them how it's done."

However, Generation Y has both the knowledge and comfort with technology the likes of which no other generation has ever seen. As a result, they have a unique opportunity to "mentor back"; to teach the older generations as much as--if not more than--the older generations have to teach Generation Y of their own experiences.

Among all of the discussion of the baby boomers and Generation Y, Generation X has become somewhat lost in the mix. Often referred to as the lost generation, Generation X consists of people born between these two generations. While they grew up among technology, they also saw it evolve. Generation Xers tend to share attitudes of the two generations they straddle.

Mark represents Generation X in our story, one who knows technology enough to assist Roger but shares some of

Roger's frustration with Phil. His frustration continues when he senses Phil taking over his territory. He finally accepts and endorses Phil when he finds a calling in the area of his passion.

Multi-Generational Mentoring

The term many people use for this concept is *reverse mentoring*, but this term is something of a misnomer. Reverse mentoring implies a complete reversal--replacing the older generation's mentoring down with Generation Yers' mentoring up. Instead, we believe the optimal solution is that each generation has knowledge that they can share with each other. Instead of reverse mentoring, perhaps the more appropriate term is *multi-generational mentoring*.

From our own experiences of multi-generational mentoring, in an organization Jeff worked for, a group had been formed to permit young professionals to network among themselves, both for social and professional purposes. The group consisted of about twenty young professionals at a lower-management level in a total workforce of about five hundred. Jeff's role at the time was the establishment of a SharePoint, an online collaboration system for the organization. They were having trouble engaging the older, "more-experienced," segment of the workforce. He met with Evan, the chair of the Young Professional group, and explained the issue. The only way he could see to get the older portion of the workforce to embrace SharePoint was to get the younger staff members, who understood the concepts and the benefits of the new technology, to act as change agents.

Evan immediately understood the issue. Together they called a meeting of the Young Professionals group. Not only did this meeting generate a large collection of great ideas but they were able to develop a strategy to send the young professionals back into their individual sections of the organization with a mission to inform and educate their older peers.

The exercise was never pitched as a mentoring program but by any definition that's what was taking place--people with experience in some aspect of business imparting their knowledge on others in a one-to-one manner. There was no formal training taking place and no defined mentoring relationship, but a somewhat covert mission being collectively carried out by committed individuals.

The organization now relies on SharePoint as its primary collaboration platform having all but abandoned traditional file-shares.

In the company Lew works for, multi-generational mentoring is practiced through the "Lunch and Learn" concept. Employees at all levels are encouraged to give presentations on some area in which they have expertise. This covers knowledge areas in technology, management, requirements gathering, how to give presentations, and many others.

The Reluctant Mentor

Attendees bring their own lunch while an "expert" gives a one-hour presentation on the meeting's topic. Employees fresh out of college give presentations on new technologies they are familiar with to coworkers whose ages range from contemporaries to aging baby boomers. The more experienced employees give presentations as well. Attendance is optional based on interest, but the audience consistently covers a broad age range.

Advantages of Multi-Generational Mentoring

- **Better leadership development.** Traditional mentoring (older down to younger) has always been an effective tool for teaching younger, less-experienced workers to accelerate their development in the business world. Allowing members of the younger generation an opportunity to share their knowledge to more experienced coworkers provides the younger professionals with leadership opportunities they will continue to build on throughout their careers. Conversely, experienced workers can further develop their own leadership skills by accepting that they are not always right or have all the answers, learning to become less authoritarian and more collaborative with diverse teams.

- **Better intergenerational relationships.** Working with more experienced workers as peers in a more collaborative environment develops stronger bonds at all levels, fostering greater tolerance of diversity and perhaps more enhanced innovation.

- **Higher employee retention rates**. Members of Generation Y want to make an impact immediately. Allowing them to mentor their more-experienced peers on topics with which they have knowledge and experience, coupled with the stronger bonds they will develop with their coworkers, provides higher job satisfaction and increases the likelihood of retention. Developing a friendship makes the interaction enjoyable and allows the mentor to feel more like a peer or colleague than a junior employee.

- **Higher organizational-wide level of technical knowledge.** The older people get, the more comfortable they become with their habits. More-experienced workers may feel like technology that is only a few years old is quite advanced whereas the younger professionals have moved on to more recent technology, such as using a flip phone verses a smartphone. Having Generation Yers share their knowledge of the newest technology with their coworkers allows the entire organization access to and benefit from the latest trends.

- **A narrower generation gap.** The ability for each generation to share its knowledge with each other results in less of an "us vs. them" attitude in the workplace. Through increased interaction and knowledge sharing, both generations will inevitably begin sharing their cultural perspectives, fostering greater understanding of each others' traditions, preferences, and ways of life. For example, each generation shares different experiences that helped shape it. Baby boomers may share their experiences of the assassinations of John F. Kennedy and Martin Luther King or the Vietnam War. Generation Xers may talk about the proliferation of AIDS while Generation Yers may talk about their childhood memory of 9/11 and the resulting fallout that changed the world.

- **Better issue resolution.** Younger mentors offer new ways to understand problems, learn, and develop ideas. Involving them in decision making provides an approach unencumbered by cynicism or assumptions that can result in more creative solutions.

- **Earlier identification of high-potential employees.** Having higher-level decision makers interacting with new employees provides upper management with earlier contact to and exposure to rising stars, allowing them to take earlier actions to ensure retention and development.

Keys to Effective Multi-Generational Mentoring

- **Acceptance of vulnerability.** It is important to be sensitive to individual differences among participants in multi-generational-mentoring relationships. The structural role-reversal requirements of multi-generational mentoring may be challenging for both mentor and mentee. Baby boomers are used to running organizations and calling the shots. They may need to be coached to question their own assumptions and consider alternative ways of thinking to allow younger coworkers to teach them.

- **Willingness to take risks.** Individuals must be willing to take risks, such as asking "dumb" questions in the learning process. Trust must be developed in each direction that mentoring is taking place.

- **Tolerance.** Each generation enters the mentoring relationship with its own biases and assumptions. Their initial instincts to each generational difference will be to resist. Each may see the other as weird and out of touch with (their own) reality. Encouraging each generation to break down the walls of intolerance of each other's culture results in opening each generation to new ideas. This was exemplified in the story when Roger realized that the younger generation had a lot to teach him.

- **Openness to sharing.** In many traditional organizations, knowledge is power. There are few incentives to sharing what one knows with others if he or she can use it to advance up the career ladder. Taking the attitude that knowledge is *information, combined with context and experience,* recognizes that the other generation has a different knowledge base due to their own context and experience, even if they have the same information available to them.

Organizations that are interested in cultivating an

environment of openness by all generations need to remove any perception that knowledge should not be shared and create incentives for sharing it. These incentives need to be supported by Knowledge Management techniques that facilitate the transfer of knowledge from the departing baby boomers to the evolving Generation Y workforce. As a result, multi-generational mentoring forms an important component of Knowledge Management.

- **Patience and Persistence.** Each generation--as well as each individual--will enter a multi-generational mentoring program with its own built-in biases. Additionally, when someone has a deep-seated knowledge of anything, he or she may become impatient when the mentee has trouble understanding. Explaining new and complex technologies to a baby boomer that has little experience with it will take persistence and understanding to help them come up to speed. Similarly, explaining cost accounting principles to a new employee without any exposure to the concept will require comparable fortitude. In our story, Roger became frustrated that Phil had not followed a budget or a timeline until he realized that Phil had no experience managing a project of that sort.

- **Starting with the right attitude.** It is important that all participants approach multi-generational mentoring with an attitude of openness. Baby boomers should not summarily dismiss Generation Yers as too inexperienced and therefore unable to teach anything. Generation Yers should not dismiss baby boomers as out of touch.

- **Keep trying.** Not everyone is a good teacher and not everyone is a good learner. Nobody is ready to learn all the time and results will vary by individual states of mind and many other factors. If someone proves that he or she is unable or unwilling to learn, work with another person. If multi-generational mentoring seems to fail with one person, it may just need more time. He or she may need to see it work successfully with others before being more amenable to it.

- **Selling instead of mandating.** If experienced workers believe in the benefits of multi-generational mentoring, they are more likely to commit themselves to such a program, resulting in greater success. This requires the organization to sell them on the idea to obtain their agreement rather than mandating their involvement in the program. Convincing them that using the technology is a more productive way to work in the twenty-first century, rather than simply adapting to Generation Y's way of doing things, may influence more buy-in with the program.

- **Building and iterating ahead of planning and defining.** The baby-boomer generation has been indoctrinated into the methods of creation through goal setting, clear definition of required outcomes, and milestone achievement. This long-term, structured planning approach conflicts with the Generation Yer who is more familiar with the Minimum Viable Product, or agile approach of simple planning, rapid creation, collaboration, and iteration. Mentoring the benefits of both methods enables an organization to capitalize on the best approach for a given situation. Roger and Mark discussed this briefly in our story in chapter sixteen while talking about website development where the agile approach enabled them to see results more quickly and adjust their requirements based on feedback.

The unique position that businesses find themselves in as more Millennials rise through the workforce is that these less-experienced workers have more knowledge about modern communication. Multi-generational mentoring allows both parties to bring knowledge and experience to the relationship. Where these relationships find their greatest value is where both parties "click" and the result is greater than the sum of the parts rather than being a simple student/teacher brain dump.

For more information and further reading on multi-generational mentoring, please go to our website at www.TheReluctantMentor.com.

CPSIA information can be obtained at www.ICGtesting.com
Printed in the USA
LVOW05s1333011114

411557LV00011BA/119/P